What people are saying abo~~

Strategies f~~

Having worked in the Industi ~~~rs, I am deeply impressed by the width and dep~ ~e key profile-raising ideas that Susan has touched upon in her book. Each idea unfolds with practical insight, workable tips and in places, academic backing. The selection of women who have been interviewed is very credible and makes the advice closer to home and real. Having spoken in many countries around the world myself, I know that key blockers for young aspiring women are many. However, what surprised me is that the core challenges remain the same across cultures. Susan has managed to capture the inner core of those issues. In a very readable, user friendly format, this book will rapidly become the go-to for young, professional women as they aspire to succeed.

Ruchi Aggarwal, Director Business Development, University of Lincoln, UK, Ex Director Marketing, Microsoft India

So many women don't realise they have the potential and often lack the confidence to rise to the top in their professions. Working in a tough and male dominated environment I understand the difficulties women face to be heard and judged as equals. *Strategies for Being Visible* is a wonderful book for emerging female leaders, full of great information and skills to help everyone raise their profiles and achieve more at work and personally.

Ann Daniels, Polar Explorer, part of the first all-female team to reach the North and South Poles

The ability to take the big picture and translate it into day-to-day, actionable strategies is the hallmark of an outstanding coach.

Sue has poured this aspect of her talent as a coach into helping women overcome self-doubt and institutional career barriers and embrace a more influential leadership role. This book is an indispensable guide for early- to mid-career women looking to accelerate their leadership development by raising their visibility. As she shares the experiences and advice of influential women leaders, Sue outlines straightforward, pragmatic steps for gaining visibility from an empowered, confident stance. Her advice covers, crucially, how to create connection at a distance using social media, writing and speaking, which is essential in the global, digitised workplace. As such, this book is a compelling addition to the toolkit of today's aspiring leaders.

Wendy Kendall, global career psychologist

For aspiring female leaders, a practical and engaging read that will support you on the path to career fulfilment, organisational change and the Leadership role you deserve. If you read one book that will support you in getting where you want to be, read this!

Michelle Farrell-Bell, CEO, Young Manchester

In this book Susan provides a unique blend of insight and wisdom into the essential skill that is raising your profile. Whether you follow all of her well-crafted strategies or pick out a few to suit, you can be assured that her easy to follow, tried and tested methods will help you gain the visibility you need to raise your career and your leadership skills to the next level.

Melanie Christie, Senior Regional Director, ICAEW

Strategies for Being Visible

14 Profile-Raising Ideas for Emerging Female Leaders

Strategies for Being Visible

14 Profile-Raising Ideas for Emerging Female Leaders

Susan Ritchie

BUSINESS BOOKS

Winchester, UK
Washington, USA

JOHN HUNT PUBLISHING

First published by Business Books, 2019
Business Books is an imprint of John Hunt Publishing Ltd., No. 3 East St., Alresford,
Hampshire SO24 9EE, UK
office@jhpbooks.com
www.johnhuntpublishing.com

For distributor details and how to order please visit the 'Ordering' section on our website.

ISBN: 978 1 78535 472 4
978 1 78535 473 1 (ebook)
Library of Congress Control Number: 2018931829

A CIP catalogue record for this book is available from the British Library.

Design: Stuart Davies

UK: Printed and bound by CPI Group (UK) Ltd, Croydon, CR0 4YY
US: Printed and bound by Thomson-Shore, 7300 West Joy Road, Dexter, MI 48130

We operate a distinctive and ethical publishing philosophy in
all areas of our business, from our global network of authors to
production and worldwide distribution.

Contents

Other Books By The Same Author

Strategies for Being Brilliant: 21 Ways to be Happy, Confident
and Successful
ISBN 978-0-904327-16-8

For the next generation – Josh, Jacob, Dan, Holly, Callum, Monroe, Isabella, Rowan, Eve and Will. May your futures all be equally bright.

Acknowledgements

This book owes a great deal to the following women who generously gave their time and wisdom.

Tiffany Hall, CIO at Cancer Research UK

Amanda Robinson, Head of Sales for Virgin Trains

Kate Turner, Head of London & South East for Lloyds Private Banking

Bronwen Batey, Former Regional Director of Marketing Communications for Banyan Tree

Heather Melville, OBE, CCMI, JP, Director of Strategic Partnerships and Head of Business Inclusion Initiatives, Corporate and Private Banking, RBS

Beverley Smith, CEO at North West Leicestershire District Council

Fiona Cownie, Professor of Law at Keele University

Jackie Daniel, NHS Chief Executive

Charlotte Sweeney, OBE, Inclusion Expert, Author and Founder of Charlotte Sweeney Associates

Tessa Shreeve, CEO of The Luxury Restaurant Guide

Sara Rees, Head of Fundraising at Rays of Sunshine Children's Charity

Caroline Welch-Ballentine, Chief Administration Officer and HRD, Richemont International Ltd

Susmita Sen, CEO Tower Hamlet Homes

Karen Friebe, Partner at Berwin, Leighton, Paisner

Kate Roebuck, Partner, Bridge McFarland Solicitors

Carol Rosati, Founder and Global Head of Inspire, Director at v2 Coaching

Kate Davies, CEO of Nottinghill Housing and CEO designate of Nottinghill Genesis

Jo Cox-Brown, Founder and Director of Night Time Economy

Jayne Mitchell, Deputy Vice Chancellor, Bishop Grosseteste

University
  Jane Scott Paul, Former CEO of the ATT
  Nicky Ness, Director of Forces Broadcasting and Entertainment
  Nicky Hill, Director of HR, Nottingham University Hospitals
NHS Trust
  Carolyn Pearson, CEO of Maiden Voyage

Foreword

Having learned so much from Sue's first book, most of which I still use today, I was eager to read her follow up. I wasn't disappointed. It's perfect if you want to take that next big step in your career but just can't get noticed.

It has down-to-earth advice with practical tools to help you AND gives examples of how other women in your situation have overcome challenges. Sue has a way of being tough and encouraging at the same time. It's her grounded approach which makes it easy to understand exactly what you should be doing and it's straight to the point. "Be bold, don't follow the rules & respectfully disrupt" - grab this book & devour it before you want to take your next big step!

Nicola Gilroy, BBC Look North

Introduction

Meet Gina.

Gina is a well-qualified professional, hard-working, ambitious and well-respected. She is reliable, trustworthy and full of ideas for growing her employer's business. She leads a team of fifteen individuals, whose performance consistently tops those of her peers. She is well-liked and committed to her role. Gina is the person her colleagues, including those more senior to her, are most likely to go to in a crisis.

She has her sights set on a regional role, and has done for the last two years.

But Gina has a problem.

She has watched as various colleagues around her have been promoted into positions she knows she could do – and do them better. She knows others are surprised that she's not yet received any of the roles she's applied for. Those roles aren't being offered to her. She is no further forward and is now beginning to lose heart. Her confidence is waning, she feels frustrated and is now beginning to doubt that she really is capable.

The fact is, Gina is great at what she does but no one sees this clearly.

Gina's profile is not high enough in her organisation. She is not visible enough. She is not sharing her skills, talents and successes because she often feels uncomfortable and thinks her work should speak for itself. Which it does – but only to a point.

Gina isn't making the impact she wants because she's not being noticed enough; she's not being seen or heard in the way she needs to be to make her next career move.

If you've picked up this book, I'm guessing it's because you may identify with someone like Gina. And you would be very typical of the kind of professional woman I've been working with for the last six years.

I decided to write this book after spotting a common theme with the women I've been working with – all of them talented, smart and ambitious women who just weren't getting the results they wanted to see.

Women who didn't know how to make themselves more visible, or if they had some idea about it, they were reluctant to do so because they felt they would be 'bragging', 'showing off' or 'blowing their own trumpet'. This made them feel uncomfortable and effectively bought their careers to a bit of a standstill – that is until we worked through strategies that could help them. Like Kathy, who had a penny-dropping moment after a workshop and went back to speak to her line manager and let her ambitions be known. The result? She was given the promotion he was asking her advice about for someone else.

Or Shona, whose hesitancy to take a promoted post involving managing former peers changed into confidence and boldness – and a new leadership position.

There are hundreds of Gina's and Kathy's and Shona's out there in business today. Women who need to know how to make themselves more visible and raise their profile so they are noticed and listened to.

And if you are one of those women, then this book is for you.

Women like you really, REALLY matter.

There are compelling economic reasons why it makes sense for women's talent to be used more effectively in the workplace. A McKinsey & Co report in 2007 (Women Matter: gender diversity, a corporate performance driver) stated that "As well as providing women with economic stability, satisfying jobs and careers, inclusive and diverse teams are more likely to be effective and better able to understand their customers and stakeholders". Further research in 2009 showed that organisations with a more equal spread of male and female board members had up to 56% higher operating profit.

In a Guardian article in 2013, Gayle Peterson, associate

fellow of Said Business School at Oxford University wrote that "If we can create change that supports more women into leadership positions and recognises their impact we may see the development of a completely new leadership identity that looks to connect with the needs of society as a whole".

And in 2011, the Davies Report concluded that at the current rate of change, it would be another 70 years before we reached gender equality on the boards of FTSE 100 companies. Another 70 years! That's not in my lifetime, or that of any woman currently working that I know. And it's not going to be in the working lifetime of any children born as you read this book either.

A 2015 update to the report recognised that although there were now more women than ever sitting on FTSE 100 boards, "More work is needed to improve the number of women to Executive Director appointments and strengthen the pipeline of women talent immediately below the board".

And that's where this book comes in.

If you are a woman who wants a first, or an early leadership role, then you are in that talent pipeline. How far you want to go is, of course, a personal choice. This book will help you whether you want to move into or stay in an early to middle leadership position, or take your talent to the top and sit on a board.

It will help you learn a set of skills in the early part of your career that you can put into practice to help you raise your profile. These are skills that will ensure that your views are heard, that you are visible in your organisation (and outside it) and that you are seen by the people that can help you to move into the role you want. Learning these skills will be one of the most helpful things you can do for yourself. They will build your confidence and empower you, give you a voice and allow you to seize the initiative in driving your career forwards.

This is important because, while the Government and industry need to address gender equality by educating everyone about unconscious bias and ensuring that cultural change within society and organisations takes place, there still falls a burden of responsibility on women themselves to be proactive in making changes.

It's not enough to sit back and wait for things to change; women need to make bold moves and learn for themselves how to feel empowered and take responsibility for their own careers. While this isn't always easy, especially if you work in an organisation or sector where the prevailing culture is one that inhibits female talent, women becoming more visible in the workplace will contribute towards a shift in practice and organisational thinking. Supporting other women to do the same, will also accelerate that shift.

Learning the skills to raise your profile and be more visible early on in your career will be one of the most crucial things you can do. Once you have found which strategies work for you, then you will have a set of tools at your disposal for the rest of your life. Not every idea in this book will appeal to everyone. Learn the ideas that feel comfortable for you – *and then use them.*

There are a range of skills that you need to succeed which include building your confidence, subject knowledge and expertise. It goes without saying that you'll be great at what you do. But to go any further in your career, you will need to know how to raise your profile and make yourself more visible. Without this, you'll be the best kept secret in your organisation - someone who can be relied on to do a great job, but not the person whose name springs to mind when it comes to a new leadership role.

How to Use This Book

In this book, I have explored 14 different strategies to raise your profile and make yourself more visible. These are all strategies I have used over the last seven years, to establish myself as a business woman in a city where I knew no one and strategies that I've used successfully with clients. The ideas in this book form one specific strand of an overall approach to building your leadership presence that I have developed over the past few years, which includes building a strong identity, developing emotional self-control, communicating powerfully, *creating a high profile* and intentionally planning to create impact in a range of settings.

I have interviewed 23 leading senior women in the UK today, from a range of industries in both public and private sectors. These are women who understand what it takes to be visible, and have attained senior roles in their careers. They have shared their reflections and experiences about what has worked for them and what they consider to be an approach that is important.

Each chapter of the book can be read on its own and dipped into. Or you may want to work your way through it in order and build on each idea. Remember, not all of them may work for you – what's important is that you find ones that feel comfortable and suit you.

The book is intended to be a useful and practical tool that you can use to help you progress your career.

I would also love to hear how you get on with the ideas. You can contact me in the following ways:

Email: hello@susanritchie.co.uk

Twitter: @susanjritchie

LinkedIn: www.linkedin.com/in/susanritchie1

Chapter 1

Make a Plan

"I made a plan for my career, just like a business plan. I took responsibility for meeting the needs of the family and then I set a career path. I thought to myself, what is there in my workplace that I have to do to get the next step up? What do I need to get there?"
Kate Davies, CEO Nottinghill Housing and CEO designate of Nottinghill Genesis

Before you go any further, you need to know where you're going, just like Kate did in the above quote.

In the coming chapters, you'll be learning about the importance of building your network and connecting with the right people – but it really helps to know who those people are. If you don't know where you're heading, it makes it practically impossible to make sure that you have the right resources around you to make it happen.

The important thing about this is that it will give you something to aim for and a solid plan of what needs to happen to get you there. It's a challenge to build a network and nurture it if you don't know who needs to be in it. And if you don't know who needs to be in it, then how are you going to find them?

It doesn't mean that you'll need your entire career mapped out in detail, cross-referenced by year and age - but it does mean that you'll need a sense of direction and the flavour of the type of roles that will interested you. This plan makes it much easier to assess whether you're heading in the right direction and creating the right opportunities regarding of who you meet and what you choose to become involved in.

It can be something as simple as sitting down and thinking about where you'd like to be two years from now. Where are you now? Do your current circumstances support your journey and what changes, if any, do you need to make? What skills do you need to develop and who do you need to be meeting and mixing with?

It's perfectly ok to do this, and put yourself first when it comes to planning for career progression. As Kate Turner, Head of London and the South East for Lloyds Private Banking says, "In a way, learn to be a bit selfish, and think to yourself, what do I need from this organisation? A lot of people think about what they can do for their organisation, which is great, but they never consider what it can do for them."

At this point it can also be a good idea to be open-minded about where your next move might be; who knows what opportunities might appear for you? If you're looking through too narrow-a-lens, you may not see the little nugget of gold that's sitting right in front of you. As Jane Scott Paul, former CEO of the AAT, explains, "In the accountancy industry, if you're ambitious then you'll want to work for one of the big four. But actually, if you work for a mid-tier firm, you'll probably get much more variation in what you're given to do and what you see."

There are some habits to get into that will support you as you move forward, and that will feed into your planning process.

Plan to Gather your Evidence

Journalling is a fantastic tool for both personal and professional development, and is something I recommend to clients. One supportive habit to get into is to make a regular note of all your professional successes and achievements. Take yourself off somewhere quiet at the end of the week and review how you've spent your time, and what impact you've made. What are your wins for the week? What contacts have you made? What potential has the week brought you? What do you intend to do with it? This is all valuable evidence to feed into your planning.

Then make a note of these things; I favour a journal, but you may like to do this electronically – it doesn't matter. What's important is that you have a record of what you've achieved that week. This is useful for you to see your progress, and when it comes to performance reviews, application forms and other situations where you may need evidence of your contributions, you'll have it all there.

A helpful extension to this approach is to find yourself a 'buddy' – someone you can meet up with maybe once a month and talk through your highlights with, as well as any challenges. You could make this a mutually beneficial exercise and help each other to celebrate achievements, reflect on performance and provide some accountability. This kind of regular professional conversation can be invaluable, as it will help you to focus on the value you add. You could even choose to challenge each other to make those achievements more visible.

Plan to Keep Up to Date

The world is a fast-moving place, and it's easy to get left behind. A little learning every day can go a long way towards keeping your knowledge current. In his excellent book, *Embodied Leadership*, Pete Hamill recommends the practice of 'deliberate reading'. This involves 20 minutes focussed reading and note-making every day, at a time when you're alert and most likely to absorb the information. Then, find ways to put this learning into practice *on the same day.*

You could read books, industry journals and magazines, websites – the choice is yours. And of course, if you prefer podcasts, videos, why not include those too? Just make sure that your reading is going to add value to what you do.

"Take the time and do this properly and you will notice a difference in your knowledge and understanding of leadership, your organisation and your industry, and so will those around you!" *Embodied Leadership, p.224.*

Try this: where do you want to be in two years' time? Use the career planning tool to help you do this.

At the end of this chapter is a career planning tool, to help you consider where you might be in two years' time, and how you can get there. Before you use it, spend a little time thinking about what's possible; make sure you get the balance right between having a plan and something to aim for, and not limiting your choices because you're aiming too narrowly.

In two years' time, I will be...
Where will I be?
What will I be doing?
Who will I be doing it with?
How will I be doing it?
Why will I be doing it?

For this to happen, in one year's time I will be...
Questions to consider:
What impact do I need to create?
How can I demonstrate my skills?
What actions will I have needed to take consistently?
Who do I need to know?
What experience will I need?
What additional knowledge do I need?
What do I need to do on a daily/weekly/monthly basis?
Where do I need to be seen?
What would I need to be better at?

For this to happen, in six months' time I will be:
Questions to consider:
What impact do I need to create?
How can I demonstrate my skills?
What actions will I have needed to take consistently?
Who do I need to know?

What experience will I need?
What additional knowledge do I need?
What do I need to do on a daily/weekly/monthly basis?
Where do I need to be seen?
What would I need to be better at?

For this to happen, right now I need to consider...
What impact do I need to create?
How can I demonstrate my skills?
How can I ensure everything I do meets my goals?
Who do I need to know?
What experience will I need?
What additional knowledge do I need?
What do I need to do on a daily/weekly/monthly basis?
Where do I need to be seen?
What do I need to be better at?

Chapter 2

Understanding Your Network

"This is the number one priority for anyone coming into the workplace or starting their own business. People will only know you if you put yourself out there - it's a conduit for having a successful career."
Heather Melville, OBE, CCMI, JP, Director of Strategic Partnerships and Head Of Business Inclusion Initiatives, Corporate and private banking, RBS.

Once you have an idea of where you're heading career-wise, then understanding, engaging with and building your network is your next task: it's all very well being visible and raising your profile, but ultimately it won't help if you have no one around you who can see you. And those people in your network will be the very people who can help accelerate your progress. At the heart of this chapter is the understanding that you need a network – a group of people who know, like and trust you, and to whom you reciprocate those feelings. A network is a two-way thing.

As Heather Townsend says in *The Financial Guide to Networking*: "You could be the most amazing employee to hire, but if no one knows about you, how are you going to be found? That's why it's so important for any professional to develop and maintain a strong network of people who can help spread the word about your services or skills."

A recent study by City University, London, concluded that professional women with leadership aspirations would benefit from understanding how to build, maintain and make use of their 'social capital' as they progressed in their careers. "These networks or 'who you know and who knows you' are responsible for a large percentage of career progression so limited access could be a barrier to women's opportunities." *Natasha Abajian, The Importance of Social Capital for Breaking the Glass Ceiling, City University, London, 2016.*

Understanding the need to build a network, how to maintain and nurture it and how to use that network, are therefore key skills for ambitious women. This is a skill that is best developed early on in your career – get to grips with it now, and you'll be building solid foundations that will support you as you move forward.

Building a network is not necessarily the same as going out and networking at a group, although that is certainly part of it. There is a place for the more formal style networking groups. Sometimes I hear from clients that they see networking as a dirty word, something that's not authentic and that feels false and uncomfortable. They may regard the idea of walking into a room and making small talk with strangers as their idea of hell, especially if they see themselves as an introvert. Seen in this light, it's little wonder that the idea of going out and networking seems about as appealing as pulling teeth to some people.

The fact is, we all have a network around us already; we just don't often recognise it as such. Think about the existing people you already know: colleagues, past colleagues, friends, neighbours, family (however distant), school, college and university acquaintances, people you've met on courses or on holiday, your partner's colleagues, the list is endless. These form a network to which you belong.

Building a network, therefore, is simply about building relationships – which for most people is a far more comfortable way of viewing it. And, given that most of us interact with at least one person a day, in some way shape or form, be it online, over the phone or face to face, then you can see that we 'network' every day. We just don't call it that.

The first step in using this idea is to widen our definition of a network away from the narrow one of simply attending groups, to one that recognises that we network all the time. Every time you speak to someone, whether you're on the train, in a shop or at a party, you are 'networking'. You are increasing the number of people to whom you are visible – which is the whole reason you've picked up this book.

This is a view that's supported by Charlotte Sweeney OBE, Inclusion Expert, Author and Founder of Charlotte Sweeney Associates. "Generally, women see networking as going to an event, but we need to change the mindset as it's not just about that; you're effectively networking all the time."

The benefit of viewing a network as a set of relationships is that you'll build more than just business contacts, as I know from personal experience. When I moved to Lincoln, where I'm currently living, I knew two people (four if you count my husband and son). Networking was something I needed to do not only to build a new business but also as a way of getting to know people and make friends. Through formal networking, I met people who shared my values and interests, people with whom I just clicked - and those people, seven years later, are now friends. And if I can help them at all in a professional sense, then I am only too happy to do that.

What's also important for a woman is to make sure that she expands that network. A recent article on the CNBC Network website stated that "Research shows that women have smaller, close-knit networks made up of people they like which makes it more challenging for women to be visible." CNBC, February 2015.

A network is a vital asset in raising your profile. You need ways to develop it and be proactive in doing so.

Know Who is in Your Network - and Keep in Touch.
To be visible to your network, you'll need to know who's in it and keep in touch with them. As your network grows, this

will become very important, but also potentially very time-consuming.

A spot of network mapping is a useful exercise for this. Grab yourself a large sheet of paper and some coloured pens; you could also use an online mind-mapping tool for this.

Draw a spider diagram in the middle of the paper and label each 'arm' with titles: friends, family, colleagues, LinkedIn contacts, past colleagues and so on. Take some time doing this, as you want a comprehensive map of who you know, no matter how distant the connection. It's only when you sit down and concentrate on an activity like this, that you will realise just who is in your network – and it will be far wider than you think.

Understanding who is in your network then allows you to make and maintain contact with them, and be strategic about it, which will be necessary as your career develops. And by strategic, I don't mean ruthless! I simply mean that in terms of your career, there will be people that you'd benefit from by being in front of - and a little planning can go a long way, as we've already seen.

Try this: carry out the network mapping activity and ask yourself the following questions, holding your career plan in mind.

Who do you need to be keeping in touch with regularly, and how can you do this?

Who else might you benefit from having in your network, that's currently missing?

How can you begin to contact those people?

Fill in the Gaps Strategically

If you know that you want to make a move into a specific sector, or a division of your organisation, then you'll need to think about how to achieve this, as the chances are, it won't just happen. This is where you'll need to be a little more strategic in how you approach things. There are going to be people that you will benefit from knowing; if you're moving up a level in your career, then you'll need to be connecting with people at that new level, so you can understand their world before you enter it.

Using events in your industry or organisation can be very helpful here in helping you to build your network while doing 'the day job' at the same time.

Tiffany Hall, CIO at Cancer Research UK, illustrates an approach she took when she attended industry conferences while working at the BBC. "I made a point of talking to other broadcasters and suppliers; a lot of colleagues just go out for dinner with other colleagues from the BBC, and I always think, you can do that in London. If we're at a trade show in Amsterdam, the people we should be talking to there are the Dutch broadcasters."

While it is often tempting to stick to people you know at events like these, the real value comes in meeting other people. Attending conferences is a great opportunity to approach people in your industry with whom you might otherwise have a very limited chance of making contact. Identify who you want to connect with, and then set about making that happen. Industry events are ideal for this, particularly if you know who's going to be there. If possible, ask for the guest list before you go.

It's an approach that Jane Scott Paul talks about: "If you're at conferences, there'll be a social element. If I was with a colleague at an important event, and there were particular people there we wanted to meet but would otherwise never get near, then we'd go through a 'hit-list' of people we wanted to speak to and divvy it up and set ourselves targets."

Nicky Ness, Director of Forces Broadcasting and Entertainment, also illustrates this approach perfectly, "You need to know who you need to know and be strategic in meeting them. I'm good at finding alternative sources of finance. I know who the decision makers are, and I once asked to be seated next to a man at a mess dinner as I knew he held the purse strings. I was able to get his support for a project and come up with a plan."

You need to be very clear about where you are networking and why. Identify who you want to network with and understand exactly what you want to achieve out of each event.

The downside of this? You can spend a lot of time and effort attending networking meetings, so it's important that you know what you want out of it. These events can be a great place to build your network to begin with, and it might be that in the early stages of your career you do spend a lot of time getting to know people at these sorts of events. Eventually, you'll need to pick and choose where you spend your time.

As Susmita Sen, CEO of Tower Hamlets Homes, warns, "For goodness sake, keep an eye on the day job. I network, but very selectively. If you're not clear about what you're doing and why, then you can be wasting your time."

One way of overcoming this is to arrange to meet people at events. You don't have to be on first name terms with people; a post in a LinkedIn group, asking who is attending xxxx conference may reveal a list of people in your industry who you can introduce yourself to. This is an excellent way of finding out if the event is worth attending in the first place, and also guaranteeing some readymade contacts for when you get there.

Another way to avoid the time that face to face networking can take up is by building a network online – as long as you don't spend all day doing this!

One of the significant advantages of an online network is that you'll be able to include influential people that you feel may be currently out of reach here. To begin with, you may not be able to meet them in person but they may have a social media account that you can begin to follow, for example, and you can start interacting with them in that way. The very act of identifying someone you'd love to meet or begin to get to know can help you to notice them in other contexts. By doing this, we send a signal to our brains which then includes that person in our filtering system called the Reticular Activating System, or RAS.

This means that we're far more likely to start noticing that person's name as we go about our daily business – which means you may suddenly begin to think how strange it is that this person is now everywhere you look! It's not strange; it's our brain's marvellous way of working – neuroscience at its most helpful.

So, aim high – don't hold back when it comes to putting people on your list of those you'd love to meet. There are ways of initiating contact and getting to know all sorts of people these days.

Try this: identify one person you'd like to have in your network and make a plan for initiating contact with them.

Managing your Network

Managing a network can become an onerous task, so find a way to keep track of who you meet, whether it's a spreadsheet of contacts, a CRM system or a 'little black book' with the details of key people in. Either way, you need to find a method that works for you.

Actively keeping in contact with people can be another job. One way to manage this is to prioritise the people that you meet. This is particularly important as your network grows and you grow in seniority. It's impossible to keep in touch with everyone all the time, but there are ways to do this that are manageable.

Using social media, such as LinkedIn and sharing regular updates can help keep you in the mind's eye of large numbers of people (there will be more on using social media later in the book), and also help you to provide value to your network by sharing useful and relevant articles and information. There will, however, also be people who you want to keep in contact with more frequently. It's worth making a note of these and forming a plan to maintain contact with them.

NHS Chief Executive Dame Jackie Daniel is quite strategic about this and works with her executive assistant to map out the people she wants to maintain contact with, putting reviews in her calendar and then working out ways to manage that contact. Meeting people for lunch is great she reflects, but realistically not always possible, so she will drop them a note, send them a card or make virtual contact.

Jackie also notes that it's important to refresh your contacts, "Sometimes you need a completely new address book and new contacts! It gets a bit stale - your network will look very different to what it was 20 years ago, and I review mine around every six months." Some people will not want to keep in contact, she also notes, and that's fine.

The main lessons here? Find a way to record who's in your network and explore different ways to keep in touch. Understand that as you move forward in your career, your network will change and you may need to concentrate on and prioritise different people. Carry out regular reviews of who you need to know, but make sure that you treat everyone you meet with respect and kindness.

Try this: identify your key influencers and be proactive in planning to keep in touch with them.

Chapter 3

Nurture Your Network

"When I was starting out, I remember talking to a young writer and thinking maybe I should be talking to her editor. Ironically, two years later, who was the editor? It was her, and she remembered me giving her the time of day - don't belittle people. She's now in charge of a big magazine, and every time we see each other, it's like meeting a long-lost friend."

Bronwen Batey, former Regional Director of Marketing Communications for Banyan Tree

Approaching networking, in whatever form, with the right mindset, is crucial.

A network is an organic entity, made up of living, breathing people with feelings, wants and needs. I'd argue that coming from a place of wanting to be helpful and of service to others in helping them meet those needs and wants, will help you to raise your profile. Ensuring that meeting your own needs ranks equally with how you can help others in your network will benefit you in the longer term. This is true wherever your network happens to be, whether it's in the formality of a networking meeting, or at a party. Generosity of spirit is a compelling trait, and you won't be forgotten in a hurry.

It can take a long time for relationships to be grown and developed, and if during that time, you're constantly thinking about what you can get out of them, then you'll be waiting a long time. It's far better to concentrate on being the kind of person that others want to get to know – from those kinds of relationships, opportunities will blossom. Show a genuine interest in people and aim to be a friend first. That's how business is done – and how you'll be remembered.

Building a reputation for this kind of approach early on in your career will stand you in good stead. Make it your default setting whatever your situation and you'll find your own profile building and strengthening as people remember what you've done for them.

It's important not to dismiss people you meet out of hand by thinking that they may not be a useful contact for you. Firstly, remember the title of this section (and Bronwen's quote), and secondly, you never know where a conversation may lead you. Every contact you make has potential benefits, if not for you personally, then it provides you with the opportunity to make a difference to someone else.

Sara Rees, Head of Fundraising at Rays of Sunshine Children's Charity, says "Building good networks is something I do from my heart."

Be generous. Be personable. Be useful.

Be a Connector of People

A great place to start is by sharing your own network – introducing contacts to each other is a generous thing to do, and shows how much you value each of them.

Heather Melville takes a similar view. "I introduce great people to each other: I'm always introducing customers to each other where they can build reciprocal business relationships. I am known for being a strong person who brings people together."

Introducing two people to each other has several beneficial effects. It provides the people you introduce with the perfect resources they need at the time; it also puts you on the radar of them both. And lastly, it provides a benefit to your network – something that should be at the forefront of your mind. This 'giving' mindset can be helpful if you're struggling with the whole concept of 'networking'.

Try this: think of two people that you know, that would benefit from an introduction to each other, and then make that happen. Aim to do this regularly, by maybe setting yourself a goal of making one introduction a week?

Follow Up

Another thing that will make you stand head and shoulders above lots of other people, and raise your profile, is if you follow up with someone after meeting them, especially for the first time. I am generally disappointed by people who don't do this. Keeping an electronic file of articles that may interest people in your industry is a useful tool; then when you meet someone, take a quick look through and send them an article that may interest them. This is a great way of keeping in touch and being useful at the same time.

You don't have to write *War and Peace,* just a short note to say how good it was to meet, maybe something complimentary about what they do, or a remark about something they've told you. The point is to demonstrate an interest in them and help them feel remembered. Mary Kay Ash, the founder of a cosmetics empire in the US, is famously quoted as saying: "Every time you meet someone, imagine they have an invisible sign around their neck saying *make me feel important.*" In the process of making others feel important, you'll be doing yourself a great favour too; you'll be raising your own profile and making it easier to be remembered and contacted in the future. Even if you meet people you know well, but maybe haven't seen for a few months, a tweet (if you're both on Twitter), or a message on LinkedIn, can be both a personal and public acknowledgement of your relationship.

It's something that Carolyn Pearson, CEO of Maiden Voyage, is a big fan of. "I really enjoy coming back from a meeting and getting a specific follow up email, or connecting on LinkedIn afterwards. 'Don't bother showing up unless you're going to follow up'. You're investing time and money in the meeting – it's a waste of both, otherwise."

Here are ten ways to follow up with someone you meet, and you can also do these periodically to help nurture your relationships:

1. Send them an email/card or simply pick up the phone and tell them how interesting it was to meet them.
2. Do one of the above and ask them a pertinent question.
3. Email a link to an article, or photocopy an article and send it to them through the post.
4. Invite them for a coffee – or if it's a good relationship you have and want to deepen, lunch.
5. Let them know about an industry event that's coming up.
6. Invite them to the industry event.
7. Introduce them to someone.
8. Refer them to someone.
9. Follow, and interact with them on social media.
10. Plan into your schedule when you'll be contacting them again.

Try this: diarise time after your next event where you know you'll be meeting new people. Try out some of the ideas above to follow up with your new contacts.

Set Up Your Own Networks

Heather Melville also invites people along to events she's organising or speaking at as a way of getting people together. With busy lives, 1:1 meetings can often be a luxury, so physically orchestrating an opportunity for your own network to meet each other can work very well. Your own profile is raised, and at the same time, you're being of service to others, which is a win-win for all concerned.

This can be something as simple or complex as:

- Inviting colleagues and peers along to a masterminding lunch.
- Setting up an internal group in your organisation with an online 'networking' space electronically.
- Launching an industry-wide group.

It's up to you to decide how visible you want to be – your visibility will grow wider with each idea.

It's something that Jackie Daniel has successfully done over the course of her career. "I've got more courageous as I've got older and more experienced. I've done more and made networks happen. I've set them up outside the NHS and in areas that overlap, and they've been hugely beneficial in showing you different approaches."

This can not only be useful to you in raising your own profile but can also be a tremendous support to colleagues and peers by expanding their own contacts and support base.

Kate Turner agrees. "When I worked at Coutts, I was involved in the founding of a woman's internal network for staff, so that female colleagues could work on their careers because the financial services industry is very male-led. I also worked on setting up an external female client network which was great for client acquisition and networking in business."

I've worked in the past with women in very male-dominated organisations, who have felt very isolated. One way of overcoming this was to contact the few other women within the organisation at management level and initiate a conversation. It's a simple way to begin a network that can be mutually supportive.

Try this: how could you form a network of your own, either within or your own organisation, or from a wider field? This could be something as simple as inviting colleagues in different departments out for lunch a couple of times a year or setting up a mailing list that shares useful resources. Seed ideas like this can lead to great things!

Meet People on a 1:1 Basis

Having 1:1 meetings with people in your network can be time-consuming but can help to deepen your relationships. It can work for you especially well inside your own organisation. This is an advanced strategy that you can use once you've firmly identified the key people you want to keep in touch with.

Two clients of mine have successfully used this over recent years. Both clients were keen to build influence in their roles; one was new to an executive role, another had been in post for some years. Taking themselves off on a 'roadshow', they both invited their fellow heads of departments/sections out for a coffee and began the process of getting to know them a little more. They found out what the priorities of their colleagues were and their current challenges. Very importantly, they asked during each meeting, how they and their team could make life easier for their colleagues. In the words of Steven Covey, "Seek first to understand, then to be understood." *The Seven Habits of Highly Effective People.*

This then allowed them to explain how they worked and what value their department could add. Both clients reported what a positive effect this strategy had on building relationships.

Try this: what can you learn from this? Who would you like to get to know a little more, and why? How could you make a 1:1 meeting happen? What questions might you want to ask – what do you need to understand? What benefits could you bring to the meeting? What is it that you'd really like them to understand about you?

Chapter 4

Step Outside Your Comfort Zone

"When I became a judge, I wasn't quite sure I could do that, and when I got this job, I wasn't quite sure I could do that either."
Professor Fiona Cownie, Professor of Law, Keele University.

Unless you can step outside your comfort zone, very few of the strategies that follow in the rest of the book will work for you. None of them involves you standing on a table and shouting 'look at me', but there is a degree of boldness about them all, in one way or another, some of which will suit you, and some of which won't. It's up to you to decide which will work the best for you.

Although this isn't a book about developing confidence, the fact is, you're going to need a reasonable level of it, and know how to manage self-doubt. I have shared some examples from the women I interviewed, to help you understand how important this idea is, and at the same time, inspire you into taking action.

Some degree of self-doubt is natural and normal when it comes to our careers, as Fiona's example above clearly shows. You can experience some uncertainty about what lies before you and still be successful if you have the right tools to help you. It certainly doesn't need to stop you in your tracks.

With the right levels of confidence, and the ability to manage moments of self-doubt, you'll be able to drive your career development in the direction you choose. Once you've left your comfort zone, whole new vistas will open up before you – but the first step is leaving it.

Tessa Shreeve, the CEO of The Luxury Restaurant Guide, remembers being pigeon-holed early on in her career. "In my 20's, in the hotel world, people saw women as being able to do sales and PR, and that was it. You had to step outside your comfort zone to move on. I never thought I would sit in front of a General Manager and sign a contract, let alone write one. But I knew inside me, that I could do it. You have to push yourself, or you'll sit where you are for the rest of your life."

This advice is still true today – nothing changes unless you do. There's a real danger that unless you're prepared to take that first step – and you can always start with a small one – you'll end up remaining exactly where you are. And for ambitious women who want to raise their profile, this won't help.

Sometimes we can never imagine where those steps might take us. Charlotte Sweeney recalls her first big move. She'd spotted an opportunity to head up a new project for Barclay's Bank in the Yorkshire region. "I'd never done anything like that before, but I put myself up for an interview and got one. I was very nervous all the way through it because I thought I was going to get 'found out' at some stage – but it was the start of where I've ended up today." That interview not only raised Charlotte's visibility, but it set her on the path she's pursued over the years.

It's worth pointing out here that often, we tell ourselves that we lack the confidence to do something, when the reality is, we're nervous. Be careful what you say to yourself! Nerves are great, it's a sign that you're stretching yourself, and about to do something that will move you up a level in your career.

In fact, getting used to feeling uncomfortable, whether that's through nerves, a little self-doubt or uncertainty about what you're doing, is something that comes with the territory.

As Jackie Daniel explains, "If you've not been uncomfortable for a while, it's a warning signal that you're not in the right place. You need to move into a place where you feel uncomfortable for a while. Women with aspirations, they need to recognise that it's part of the deal."

And that's what you are – a woman with aspirations. So, accept that you'll need to feel uncomfortable; it's part of the process. Accept that you can feel nervous and self-doubting; it's part of the process. And accept that you're certainly not alone in this; it's part of the process for everyone.

In the next section, we'll look at examples of how to move out of your comfort zone. You'll hear some inspiring stories of women who've made bold moves, which illustrate just why this is such a fundamental approach to raising your profile.

How to Move Out of Your Comfort Zone

Understand your Strengths

One of the most useful tools you can possess as a woman in business is an understanding of your strengths and skills. This allows you to play to them; you can't be great at everything. Once you know what your strengths are, this allows you to build a team around you, made up of people whose strengths complement yours.

Understanding your strengths also makes it easier to leave your comfort zone, as it can be a tremendously useful confidence-building tool. It allows you to state clearly, 'I am a woman who...' When you're able to say this to yourself and then to others, it opens doors for you because it allows for possibility. Our brains are hardwired to look for evidence to back up our self-perceptions; self-consistency theory prompts us to look for examples that prove we are who we say we are, and so we tend to act in ways that keep us consistent with that self-image. If you tell yourself that you are a woman who takes risks, for example, you'll be far more likely to take some. The same can work in reverse though – so if you're busy telling yourself you don't like change, for instance, then the chances are you'll end up resisting change.

Deliberately focusing on what you're good at can help to build confidence, which can influence how you behave; it's never too late to change how you're thinking. The field of

Neuroscience research is showing us that our brains demonstrate neuroplasticity – this means that our brains are capable of structural change, with repeated practice at something. It requires practice and commitment – but the possibilities for re-wiring ourselves with new, more positive and supportive habits are exciting.

When it comes to understanding your strengths, it's important to keep track of things - you'll develop skills as you progress in your career, and you'll gain experience of different situations. This can be especially helpful when it comes to stepping up and applying for roles that you may not have previously thought of, or for roles that don't immediately seem to have your name on them.

In Chapter 1, I mentioned the usefulness of keeping a professional log; keeping a note of every project that you get involved in, and analysing what skills you've either built on or developed from scratch can help here. This is also useful because it allows you to see where you've got gaps in your experience too.

Beverley Smith, the CEO of North west Leicestershire District Council, has used this strategy throughout her career. After leaving a nine-year career with the police, including a five-year stint in the CID, she worked her way up in a series of local authority roles, to where she is now, as a Chief Executive Officer. She did this without any professional qualifications, other than the degree she left university with (apart from a recent coaching/ mentoring qualification).

"After I left the police, I decided I would start my career again in local government. I had no understanding or experience of it, but I thought about what skills I did have, that I could take with me. I've never gone to any job with previous experience – I've always gone with generic skills. I joined as a fraud investigator, then led a new team, then became a planning enforcement officer and my career progressed from there."

Beverly has a clear understanding of what she can do – and is obviously able to articulate that very well. This is what you should be aiming to do too – understand what you can do well, and be able to demonstrate what this means in practice. This means being able to analyse, interpret and apply your experience in a range of different settings so that your value is crystal clear.

This will give you the confidence to make moves that take you outside your immediate realm of experience and help you to be seen through a new lens by people who may not have recognised some of your skills previously.

Know what skills, strengths and talents you have, and understand what they enable you to do with them.

Try this: see your own experience through the lens of Beverley's example. Carry out a skills and strengths inventory by reviewing your own performance, and asking others what they think are your key ones. Identify the skill and say what it means that you're able to do. Ask yourself 'so what?' – What's the impact of you having this skill? If you're not already doing so, get into the habit of having a weekly review of all your accomplishments and achievements too; this is useful material to have to hand.

Grow some Self-Belief

Once you have identified what your top skills and talents are, then you need to be able to use them and talk about them. Moving out of your comfort zone necessitates that you can do this. Permitting yourself to go after opportunities means that you're far more likely to do so. Often, it's that unhelpful little voice that tells us we're not good enough, that stops us in our tracks. Silencing that will help you to move out of your comfort zone and begin raising your profile.

Carol Rosati OBE, Founder and Global Head of Inspire, and Director at v2 Coaching, has an approach that builds upon Beverley's experiences. "I often say to women, take off your modesty blanket and put away your blinkers and write yourself a sales pitch. List 10 things that you're proud of. Learn the pitch and throw it away. You'll come across as self-assured and comfortable in your own skin."

What underpins this, is growing self-belief. When we believe we can do things, we subtly demonstrate that to the world, by changing the way that we show up in it – and this changes what others see when they look at you.

It's an approach that Kate Davies used early on in her career in housing. When her manager told her that he'd got to re-write a development strategy, but didn't have time, Kate didn't hesitate to volunteer even though she'd never written one before. "I just looked at the guidance about what you had to write, brought together the information and wrote something that was quite good and he was a bit surprised."

Kate had spent two years learning as much as she could about the industry she'd chosen to work in; for her, the knowledge she'd gained in that two years of focussed learning and research, coupled with the self-belief that she could produce something worth reading, paid off. Here's a real example of throwing off the modesty blanket – Kate needed to understand her own skills and strengths first, and importantly, where the gaps were. This is crucial; truly understanding what you are capable of will allow you to move from your comfort zone and into a position where you can impress others.

If you're busy denying your talents to yourself, then you'll have a tough time with this. There is no place for self-delusion. A belief in yourself first allows you to demonstrate that to others.

Remember – it's impossible to demonstrate your value to others if you cannot see it yourself.

Try this: practice throwing off your modesty blanket! If you've understood what your skills and talents are, then you'll be able to make a list of 10 things that you're proud of. Memorise that list. Even if you choose not to share that list verbally with others, then the memory of it will be carried with you. Thinking about what's on the list can affect your physiology, your posture, your tone of voice and general demeanour.

Be a 60%er

It's well documented that men will apply for jobs when they meet 60% of the criteria, while women will wait until they meet 100% of it.

A recent HBR article, *Why Women Don't Apply for Jobs Unless They're 100% Qualified*, makes the point that although these statistics are usually put down to a lack of confidence on women's part, research carried out by Tara Mohr indicates another reason. Both men and women in her survey identified their number one reason for not applying for a role when they didn't meet all the criteria, as being "I didn't think they would hire me since I didn't meet the qualifications and I didn't want to waste my time and energy."

The article points out that it's the mistaken assumptions women make about the application process that stops women applying for roles where they don't meet all the criteria.

"They didn't see the hiring process as one where advocacy, relationships or a creative approach to framing one's expertise could overcome not having the skills and experiences outlined in the job qualifications."

Once the penny drops, it's "…a wake-up call that not everyone is playing the game that way. When those women know others are giving it a shot even when they don't meet the job criteria, they feel free to do the same." *HBR August 2014*

You need to leave your comfort zone and apply for those roles where you don't meet all the criteria *because other people are – and you probably have enough confidence to do the job*. It's ok to do this; giving yourself permission not to play by the 'rules' is the important point here. If you have people-pleasing tendencies or are a rule-follower, then this can be a challenge at first. But please bear with it – it's worth stepping out of your comfort zone and taking that risk.

I was bought up to be a rule-follower – a good girl who did as she was told. In many ways, this has served me well. I am personable, easy company, well-liked, a safe pair of hands… someone who can be relied upon to do an excellent job. However, slavishly following the rules is career-limiting.

I remember following the newly created Literacy and Numeracy Hours to the letter as a teacher in the early 1990. I felt cheated some years later when those teachers who threw the rule book out of the window, convinced that they could teach those subjects better, did so – and got great results. It changing the way we taught.

It taught me a lesson in how change comes about, and it wasn't from the rule-followers like me. Change happens because there are people out there who intentionally say no, and decide that not all of the rules need to be followed. They don't ask permission but use their judgement to shake up the status quo.

This is my message to you – you don't have to follow all the rules. Other people don't.

And if you're still not convinced, then read what Jo Cox Brown, Founder and Director of The Night Time Economy, has to say about it.

In previous roles, she would tell her team that any of them should apply for roles if they can do 60% of the specification for it. The other 40%, she advocates, is where your growth lies.

"None of us wants to go into a job and say I can do it all because you'll be bored. You need to be able to do 60% of it, and the other 40% is your opportunity to put yourself on courses, to seek people out to invest in you and to create a plan to develop. When you get to 100%, it's time to move on to a new challenge; otherwise, you're stopping the next person coming up behind you from getting to that stage."

Framed like this, becoming a 60%er is being not only helpful to your own career but beneficial to others too.

Try this: look at the jobs currently on offer in your industry. How many of them could you meet 60% of the criteria for? What skills and experiences have you got that you could use to demonstrate how you could meet the other 40%? How could you stretch yourself to meet the demands of the new role? The real skill here is in framing your talents correctly – how can you do that?

Don't be so Agreeable

By this, I don't mean for you to develop a disagreeable personality. What I'm getting at here is the need to develop your own opinions about things, rather than simply reiterating the opinions of others. This is an area where self-doubt can reign supreme if we're not careful, and it's a big step outside a comfort zone for many women.

But it's also a necessary one.

Cultivating an opinion about the key issues in your team, your organisation and your industry will help you to become more visible – but that's only if you can bring yourself to share them in the first place. In Chapter 1, I made the point that keeping yourself up to date with what's going on is a pre-requisite – make sure you read industry journals and articles, and keep an eye on industry leaders, so you're fully informed.

Then start opening your mouth and telling people what you think. Resist the urge to simply validate and back up the opinions of colleagues – even if you happen to agree with them.

Professor Jayne Mitchell, the Deputy Vice-Chancellor of Bishop Grosseteste University, advises that women shouldn't give away their own opinions by hiding them inside someone else's. "Women sometimes give more oxygen to validating the point of someone else rather than getting to the point that they'd really like to be making – you don't need to agree with what the previous person has said all the time. You don't need to build on someone else's point; it's much better to make your own point straight out."

The danger here is that if you reinforce someone else's point, you'll sound as though you don't have your own voice. Even if you do agree with someone, you can still put your views across in your own way. Resist the urge to start with the words 'I agree with...' and instead make your own point concisely and clearly, at a measured pace, using language that carries impact.

One approach that is very useful to cultivate, and can take a little time to develop, is that of speaking authoritatively. This involves eliminating phrases like 'I think' and 'I believe' and stating your opinions as fact. This is a strong mode of communicating and packs a lot of punch; the result of this is that you will end up with people disagreeing with you – often vehemently so. The more visible you are, the more this will happen.

You'll need to expect this. You'll also need to understand that it won't be personal. As Jo Cox Brown says: "We can't please everyone all of the time – and if we are, we're doing it wrong. None of us are called for people pleasing – we're called for a mission, or for something we want to achieve, and if we follow that line, then it stands to reason we're going to disrupt someone or upset them."

Acknowledging your intention here matters. You need to understand that your intention is not to upset others but to achieve your vision. People won't always agree with you; you need to learn to trust yourself and understand that you're making decisions based on your own skills, experiences and knowledge and that your opinion is as valid as anyone else's. As Sara Rees says, "Trusting my instincts and having the courage of my convictions was a huge step outside my comfort zone." You can do this too.

You won't achieve that vision though if you're motivated by getting people to like you and agree with everything you say. The fact is, the people that get noticed the most are those who have their own voice, are willing to use it and have the courage to pursue their own ideas.

Nicky Ness is someone who's not been afraid to challenge the normal way of doing things. Sometimes, taking action that goes against what everyone else is doing can push us out of our comfort zone it's true, but what lies outside it can be extremely rewarding.

"Disturb the norm is my view because you never quite know what you'll find. If you do it in an emotionally mature and respectful way, you'll stand out from other people." When she started her career in radio, Nicky chose not to write stories in the same way as other presenters. "I stood out because I just didn't tread the path everyone else did. After three months the guy who took me on told me I'd go far in the organisation."

By leaving your comfort zone and doing things differently, you'll raise your profile simply by being different. The examples in this chapter highlight the need for taking action that helps you to push yourself out of your current boundaries. You need to be prepared to do this, to make the most of the ideas in the next chapter – spotting and seizing opportunities.

Try this: practice being disruptive – in a respectful way. What ways can you find that will challenge the status quo and bring a fresh perspective to the usual ways of doing things? When was the last time you shared your own opinions about an issue in your industry or organisation? How can you tread a different path to others?

Chapter 5

Spotting Opportunities and Seizing Chances

"One day I stood up to do an event, and I realised there were 60+ men staring at me. The only other woman in the room was a waitress topping up glasses. It was such a slap in the face, and I thought, wow, seriously? That's how INSPIRE was born."
Carol Rosati OBE, Founder and Global Head of Inspire, Director at v2 Coaching

Opportunities are all around us – we just need to see them for what they are and be prepared to do something with them.

This is a crucial skill, which relies on several things – awareness, confidence, a willingness to take risks and a vision for your personal future that stretches beyond where you may be now. A creative and innovative mind is also necessary, one that can think laterally and is agile.

Why?

Because without the ability to spot opportunities, you'll be forever where you are. Without the motivation to seize any chances, you'll never make the most of those opportunities. Learning to spot opportunities and seize them can give you new skills, open up fresh, useful networks and help you to build a platform for yourself while at the same time benefitting others. Constantly being aware of what's going on around you will help you to drive your career forward by identifying your next steps. Couple this with being proactive, and you can take your career in some exciting, previously unthought-of directions, putting you in the path of people whom you may never otherwise have met. This can change the trajectory of your career.

Opportunities won't just land in your lap (or rarely will), and sometimes necessity dictates that we need to find our own. Carol Rosati's quote at the top of this chapter illustrates perfectly how an opportunity can present itself – as long as you have your eyes open and can see it. She's a great example of what can happen to women who are aware enough to see a need, and bold enough to take action. The Inspire network now links over 5,000 women across four continents, from its first event in 2008. Carol has extended her work to visiting schools to effect change in education, starting cultural change at an early age, and she has been awarded an OBE. All this grew from making an observation at a speaking event.

You can learn to spot opportunities like this, if you are open to them. Carol was proactive in following up the opportunity she spotted. With the right mindset and self-belief, you can do this too. Your opportunities may be on a smaller scale to begin with, but it's a practical way to demonstrate your talents so that they speak for themselves.

And spotting an opportunity won't go unnoticed.

Jane Scott Paul's philosophy is that leadership exists at all levels in an organisation and doesn't just reside in those with the title. There are leadership opportunities in every team you may be in. She noticed this in the call centre of the ATT, which was an entry-level position in the organisation. She could spot 'star quality' within weeks of someone starting – simply being curious and asking questions marked someone out as having potential.

She recalls a young temp who came and spoke to her and told her that he'd really like a permanent job there. "I asked him what he was interested in and he gave me a list of things some of the departments did. I told him to go and introduce himself and ask if there were any opportunities. I thought he was incredible for knowing what he wanted and doing something about it. He ended up with a permanent job and a promotion too."

You never know who will be watching and noticing you.

In the next section, we'll talk about how, and what sorts of opportunities you may be able to find and hear from other women who have seized their own, with impressive results.

Horizon-scanning

Firstly, remain alert. As with the example of Carol Rosati, if you're not looking, you'll never see anything! This can be mean being open to seeing opportunities within your organisation or your wider industry. Keeping up to date with industry news will allow you to stay ahead of any changes – and with change comes opportunity. This could be in the form of legislation, innovations or staff turnover.

This is an approach that worked well for Beverley Smith. She says, "Know the environment, and what's coming up on the horizon. Earlier on in my career, the person leading a problem service in the authority walked away, so I spoke to the right person and said I could turn it around. I didn't just say 'give it to me', I went with ideas. Part of this is doing your homework and research so that you're credible when you're trying to get yourself heard."

Charlotte Sweeney has used this tactic to great effect too. "Throughout my career, I've thought about two things. As soon as I've got one job, I've been focussed on doing it brilliantly – and then, what's my next job?"

Both examples show the need for awareness, research and planning when it comes to your career, as well as a proactive mindset that enables action to be taken. Horizon-scanning can help you to be visible in areas that you may not have considered previously.

Try this: ask yourself how much you know about what's going on in your industry or organisation. How up to date are you about developments, and how can you find a source of information that you can tap into regularly? What are the key roles or opportunities on the horizon that you could possibly become involved in? What research might you need to do, and how you could do this?

Saying Yes

The nature of opportunities sometimes means that they may slip away before we have time to consider them. One way to combat this is to develop the ability to say 'yes', and then work out the details later. This does mean being very aware of what's around, as in the previous point, and knowing the benefits of the opportunity on offer, so that when it presents itself, we can seize it without too much delay. There may well be obstacles we need to overcome before we can take advantage of what's on offer – so this is where a problem-solving mindset and some tenacity and determination come in.

If an opportunity is worth seizing, then it's worth making some effort for. Charlotte Sweeney described actively seeking out an opportunity to work at a branch of Barclays where she knew she would get some valuable experience, even though it would increase her daily commute by two hours each day. The message here is not to be put off by barriers, which is an attitude that will make you stand out amongst your peers.

Tessa Shreeve shares this mindset. She sees an opportunity in everything and says "Others give up so easily. I find if you go beyond that point of giving up, then you totally take people by surprise. I've swung about 50% of contracts round when people have said no - there's an opportunity in every challenge."

Both Charlotte and Tessa are tenacious and determined. Do you share their characteristics?

Try this: how 'yes' ready are you? Do you know enough about what's going on around you that you've identified a few opportunities you'd be ready to say yes to, regardless of how you're going to make them happen?

Be Creative

In the same way that Carol spotted an opportunity earlier on in this chapter, Tessa was also able to identify a way to make changes in her industry and sought out a creative way to make those changes happen, against the odds. After leaving a global role in the hospitality industry, Tessa realised that there was a different way to do business. Her competitors were international market leaders with a lot of resources and spending power, in comparison to her fledgling company. Her answer? To approach a university and ask to pitch her project to the students and see if they could build her a CRM database.

By using her initiative, there were mutually beneficial outcomes, for both her and the students. She managed to grow her business at the same time that the students were using her project as part of their thesis. "It was all about thinking around problems that were presented, not taking no for an answer and finding a solution for it all. I knew I could do a better job than my former company and I went for it." The result? She ended up with a great database that allowed her company to grow over a five year period, to the stage that she could afford to buy something bigger and better.

Creativity is a highly valued trait and often one that is encouraged in organisations. The adhesive company 3M is a great example of this. For example, they allow employees 15% innovation time to develop new ideas, which cannot easily be taken away. A Harvard Business Review article, *'The Innovation Mindset in Action: 3M'*, concludes that "The innovation mindset is a game-changing asset for companies as well as individuals." *HBR 2013.*

Often, the opportunities are right under our noses – we need the right conditions and clarity of vision to help us see them. Every system or process can benefit from improvements at some point, and your industry or organisation will no different. Generating innovative ideas that may potentially drive efficiencies or benefit customers or colleagues in some way, will raise your profile no end.

What are you waiting for?

Try this: value creativity. Follow the example of 3M, and spend some time every week thinking about how you could improve processes or procedures within your organisation. In this way, you'll generate your own opportunities and be massively involved in seizing them too. Then – who could you share these ideas with, and how?

Involve Yourself – Whether you're Invited or Not

Social media is a great place to practice horizon-scanning and spot opportunities. Anyone can become involved in public tweets, posts and updates. It's an ideal opportunity to involve yourself in discussions, whether you're part of it to begin with or not. Opportunities will literally appear in front you as they move through the timeline of whatever social media account you're using.

Watch out for people asking questions, or Twitter chats, for example, around pertinent topics in your industry. Because of the social nature of social media, you can easily join in with a debate and add your opinion.

Jackie Daniel did this. "I managed to get myself central to a female network that's just been set up in the NHS by the Health Service Journal. I just got in the middle of a conversation that I thought I could contribute to. I wrote an article that they used extensively to promote the leadership network, got myself on a debate to launch it, and that put me in contact with a whole variety of people I've not met before."

Here, a combination of spotting the opportunity and seizing it, is what's important. The conversation didn't just end there, on social media – Jackie followed up on it by writing an article that proved pivotal to her whole experience of raising her profile in this way. Similarly, I was once tweeted by a woman's organisation about an upcoming webinar. Instead of registering for it, I tweeted them back and asked if they would like me to run one for them – this led to a chat over the phone and my own webinar event.

Another useful approach to take here is to look out for opportunities for others and be proactive in either alerting people to those opportunities, or recommending a contact. Being genuinely generous and thoughtful will go a long way towards raising your profile and help build a reputation you can be proud of.

Try this: do some horizon-scanning on whatever social media channels you use, and keep your eyes open for opportunities to become involved in debates and conversations. What value can you add? Connect with the people you're talking to and then follow up the conversation in some way. Don't be afraid to put yourself forward for things; can you also find opportunities for colleagues and peers? Set yourself a challenge to see if you can find one opportunity for yourself and one for someone else each month.

Look Outside the Workplace

This next idea is a great one for really broadening your profile outside of your organisation and, at the same time, develop your skills and make a difference to your community.

It's important to develop an awareness of yourself as a leader. This means understanding your skills and talents, including where you need to improve them. Your workplace may not be able to provide everything you need to grow and develop yourself, in which case, you'll have to look elsewhere. This can also provide you with opportunities to raise your profile in a completely different sector.

Jo Cox Brown illustrates this superbly. Her philosophy is that if there are things she can't get in the workplace, then she looks to get them by serving a charity, her local community or by starting something up outside of work. This is about being strategic and thinking about where you could get your experience from.

"I didn't have much experience of chairing meetings, so I took the chair of a charity in Ghana, who work with young women escaping the sex trade. I did that for about two years and got experience in chairing multi-disciplinary meetings."

Any kind of volunteering can work for you in terms of raising your profile and giving your CV vital skills and experience. A client of mine was applying for her first promoted post and felt she lacked the skills in managing budgets that were asked for. However, her involvement in running a local youth organisation meant that she did have a small budget to oversee. There was her budget experience – not in work admittedly, but she was able to demonstrate she had the skills, and talk about them at her interview.

There are opportunities outside of work to develop yourself, while at the same time, making a difference to a charity or social enterprise. This will bring you into contact with people in different sectors, and those skills you end up with will help raise your profile back in the workplace too; firstly, because you have them, when your peers may not, and secondly because you've been proactive in acquiring them.

Try this: where do you lack either skills or experience? Where could you volunteer that might help you to develop this missing expertise? Find somewhere that matches your interests and personal values.

Chapter 6

Volunteering for Projects

"I've never been shy of volunteering - I know I can do a good job, but it's a question of showing them. Your reputation is built on delivery, so you need to manage the 'yes's' and choose the right ones."

Beverley Smith, CEO of North West Leicestershire District Council

As you've already discovered, volunteering for projects is an excellent way of raising your profile and becoming more visible, if done correctly. This chapter contains some ideas on how to get that right.

Let me start by telling you a story. Not all projects to volunteer for are created equal.

In my previous career as a teacher, I was the literacy manager for the school I worked in when I lived in Asia. This meant organising the annual book week. I spent a considerable amount of time setting up interesting and fun activities for the children and staff, reading stories and dressing up as book characters; if you've got children, I'm sure you'll know exactly what I mean!

I had a colleague, who at the same time, had volunteered to organise an international conference. While I was busy reading books to the children, she was busy talking to the authors of some of those books, liaising with international schools and other organisations and getting herself on the radar of much larger fish than were in my pond.

Now there's nothing wrong with organising a book week, please don't get me wrong; it's a great thing to do. But with a profile-raising head on, can you see that the international conference, or something similar, would have been a better choice for me?

You may have volunteered for things like this yourself, and wondered afterwards, exactly what you've got out of it – you put lots of effort in, but the personal rewards are slim.

It's important to ensure that anything you volunteer for has a distinct career benefit for you, as well as a business benefit for your organisation. Finding the sweet spot where the two overlap takes some skill and discernment, and maybe some negotiating, but it's crucial.

As Beverley says, "Sometimes you can say yes to something that won't get you any further on in terms of recognition or networks, so I'm careful about the ones that have the biggest influence for me as well as the council."

I didn't make the same mistake twice. After leaving teaching, I joined a networking group and within nine months was sitting on the leadership team. This gave me great exposure in leading and running meetings. However, it was my next volunteer position that really worked to my advantage. As the education officer, my role included delivering bite-sized training once a week for a year – a superb opportunity for me to stand up in front of a room full of business leaders and show them exactly what I could do. This was a win-win for all concerned – myself, the networking organisation and its members too.

Before you rush to volunteer for the next thing that comes along, take some time to consider how much benefit is there for you *as well as* your organisation. Of course, it's a good idea to make sure that you're making the most of current experience and skills too.

How to Identify Volunteering Projects

Be Strategic
When it comes to using volunteering for projects as a profile-raising tool, make sure you understand what you need to further

your career and look for projects that will add to this for you. Make sure that you've completed the career mapping exercise at the beginning of the book to help you with this. Look at the jobs above you on your career path, and then review your CV. If one of those jobs came up, would you have the necessary skills? What's missing?

Beverley explains further, "Earlier on in my career, knowing other Chief Execs outside Nottingham was limited because I wasn't a Chief Executive. As the deputy, I didn't get to go to conferences and things like that, so I contacted the LGA and asked them, and my own CEO if I could be a peer reviewer. I then went into different authorities to provide support to them, and I travelled all over the country doing that. It benefitted my own authority because of the learning I took back to them, and it benefitted me in terms of my profile and being able to mix with the right people. It's that type of thing you have to be clever about."

It's also important to be strategic in terms of expanding your skill set. Taking on projects that use existing skills without stretching you will have limited value in developing yourself professionally. It's also too easy to get pigeon-holed; adopting the same type of role may not always be helpful for you if it's one that is more supportive, for example organising and arranging. High profile projects are ones that often break new ground, and if you want to become more visible, it's an idea to push yourself and take on a more demanding role. This means that you'll likely be challenged at various points during the project, but you'll have a valuable set of skills at the end of it.

Your contribution to your organisation is important too; they're going to benefit more from having you develop your skills in this way.

It's something that made Sara Rees re-evaluate her tendency to volunteer for similar projects.

"A colleague told me I should think more carefully about the projects I was taking on. It was a good lesson for me to think a little more carefully and to think bigger and better each time and to take on something chunkier. Your organisation won't be getting the best out of you if you're constantly punching below your weight in what projects you take on."

A word of warning here though. While it's great to be stretched and develop new skills, it's important to make sure you have the capacity to take on any new projects, both in time and your abilities. Your reputation depends on your ability to deliver - so make sure you can!

Try this: carry out a skills audit using the Skills Audit tool at the end of the chapter and review your network mapping exercise from earlier. Where can you identify gaps? What specifically do you need to work on developing or who do you need to be meeting? Review any projects currently on offer in your organisation – do they match your needs?

Understand What's Important

Hand in hand with the previous strategy comes this; understanding what's important to the people who are likely to promote you. What do you need to be able to do really well in order to succeed? You'll need this information whether you're looking to be promoted internally or externally. Understand what is valued and then look for projects that can either build that skill in you or help you to demonstrate it to a wider audience.

Once you understand this, then you can work on developing that by getting training and experience and building your knowledge base around it. Fiona Cownie says, "In academia it's publications. If you identify that, then you have really got to go for that because you've got to give yourself enough confidence that you can compete with anybody in that area."

Try this: review your industry or organisation. What are the key skills that are valued and how do you match up to those? Where do you need more training or knowledge? If you already possess a good level of skill, how can you move beyond good to great?

Skills Audit

Use the grid below to highlight your current skills, and the potential skills you will need to take the next step up in your career. There are two ways you can do this; use a highlighter to mark the 'Current' column in one colour, and use a different colour to highlight the 'Potential' column. Where do the columns match up? These are areas where you have the required skills for your potential move. Your current skills may not always match your potential ones; these are areas for development.

Another way to use the grid is to focus on the 'Potential' column, identify the skill you're going to potentially need and score yourself out of 10 for that skill.

1 = I don't have that skill at all, 10 = I couldn't get any better at it.

For example, if 'facilitation' is a potential skill you'll need in your next move, and it's something you don't have a great deal of experience in, you may score yourself a four. You may then set yourself a goal to move to a six, for example, by a given date.

Your grid may look like this:

Figure 1.

Current	Potential
Facilitation	Facilitation
4 ——————————————————⟶ 6	

You can then plan to bridge the gap between the four and the six; what do you need to do to reach the score of six?

The grid contains common generic skills; you may want to add your own set of skills that may be unique to your industry.

Skills Audit Grid

Current	Potential	Current	Potential	Current	Potential
Making decisions	Making decisions	Punctuality	Punctuality	Writing	Writing
Public speaking	Public speaking	Organising people	Organising people	Assessment	Assessment
Being objective	Being objective	Seeing an overview	Seeing an overview	Drawing conclusions	Drawing conclusions
Adaptability	Adaptability	Persuasion	Persuasion	IT skills	IT skills
Social media	Social media	Negotiating	Negotiating	Time management	Time management
Organising resources	Organising resources	Motivating	Motivating	Interpersonal skills	Interpersonal skills
Initiating projects	Initiating projects	Completing projects	Completing projects	Giving presentations	Giving presentations
Facilitation	Facilitation	Observation	Observation	Crisis management	Crisis management
Risk taking	Risk taking	Following instructions	Following instructions	Giving instructions	Giving instructions
Emotional intelligence	Emotional intelligence	Networking	Networking	Coaching	Coaching
Telephone skills	Telephone skills	Sales	Sales	Creating rapport	Creating rapport
Diagnosing	Diagnosing	Predicting	Predicting	Ideas generation	Ideas generation
Finances	Finances	Goal setting	Goal setting	Interpretation	Interpretation
Listening	Listening	Resilience	Resilience	Using intuition	Using intuition
Attention to detail	Attention to detail	Planning	Planning	Evaluating	Evaluating

Chapter 7

Be Memorable

"Then something happened that stays with me even now and I think this is the secret to how I've progressed in the organisation. It's part of a legacy that people still talk about now."

Nicky Ness, Director of Forces Broadcasting and Entertainment

Being memorable – what a double-edged sword this can be! On the one hand, it's crucial – who wants to be forgotten and make the impact of a damp squid – but on the other hand, get this wrong, and it's possibly the end of any career progression in the particular circles you're moving in. As Caroline Welch-Ballentine, Chief Administration Officer and HRD for Richemont International Ltd told me, "One person's memorable can be another person's complete disaster!"

Your reputation goes before you – and it's up to you to make sure it's the reputation you want to have. It's the same with the impact you want to make; not thinking your approach through or behaving in an off-guard manner at the wrong moment can have serious consequences.

Let me explain a little more.

The horns and the halo effect refer to our tendency as human beings to make quick judgements about others, based on a limited range of evidence. We interpret that evidence through the lens of our own values and preferences; this bias means that we may ascribe qualities to people that simply don't exist. Although Edward Thorndike, the psychologist who coined the term 'halo' effect in the 1920s, originally referred to people and their levels of attractiveness, studies have shown that this occurs in a wide range of fields from politics, business and education.

So how does it work?

Let's imagine a member of my team, Sally, is always early to meetings. Punctuality is a key value of mine, and I love the way Sally matches this. The fact that she's early signals to me that she is reliable, cares about the team, is committed and trustworthy.

On the other hand, Sandra has been late for the last three meetings. I can't stand lateness; I look at Sandra, and I *know* that she's unreliable, a shoddy worker, selfish and untrustworthy.

What I don't know is that Sally is always there early to gossip, try and manipulate her superiors and pick up information to her advantage. Sandra is late because she's the last one in the office, left to troubleshoot problems that have arisen and cope with a last-minute crisis.

Can you see how this phenomenon can influence others about you? It means that if you're being viewed through the halo lens, not only will people think more positively about you, but you're more likely to be forgiven for minor transgressions. The opposite is true for the horns lens; if others have a negative view of you, they'll constantly look for confirmation of their opinion. You ignore it at your peril.

It's tied up closely with your reputation, and while we can't dictate what others think and say about us, we can have some influence over those areas so that we maximise the chances of being memorable for the right reasons.

Here's some ways to do that.

How to be Memorable

Understand Other People's Values
Avoiding the horns and the halo effect can be quite simple if you're prepared to put your powers of observation to the test. The horns and halo lenses reflect our values and preferences, meaning we have a bias towards certain types of behaviours and attitudes in others. By understanding the values of the people around you, and what's important to them, you can avoid

invoking the horns effect as much as possible by not offending their values and affirming them instead.

If you know, for example, that your boss dislikes lateness, then for goodness sake be on time for meetings with her. Simple. If you're someone who runs late constantly, and you don't see anything wrong with that, then this may be a challenge for you – but this isn't the time to focus on your preferences. It's about understanding what matters to someone else and reflecting that behaviour and attitude back to them as far as you're able. It's not about pretending to be someone else though, or something you're not, as we'll discuss a little later in this chapter.

Try this: take some time to listen to and observe those people around you. What do they reveal through their communication? When I was training to be a coach, we were told that people will tell you everything you need to know if you observe well enough. It's true! What matters to those around you? What do they talk about and what does this tell you about them? Observe and reflect; what values are being revealed and how can you make sure that you affirm those values as you interact with them on a daily basis?

Be Aware of the Energy You Bring with You

Have you ever been able to look at someone you know well, a family member, a friend or a close colleague, and instantly guess their mood? What you're doing at this moment is picking up on their energy levels.

Our energy is revealed in subtle ways through our body, and we're often not aware of it – the set of our face, the way we walk and talk and hold ourselves, our physiology and posture all communicate messages to the room we're in, long before we open our mouths.

By focusing on how we want to feel and adjusting our intentions and physiology, we can change the energy we bring with us. Something as simple as stretching, standing taller and even smiling if we don't feel happy have all been proven in studies to reduce the intensity of the body's stress response. If you've not watched the great TED Talk by Amy Cuddy, *Your Body Language Shapes Who You Are*, I suggest you Google it, as it's a great example of how we can change our mood through changing our bodies – and therefore changing the energy with which we show up.

The other way to change the energy we bring to a situation is by deliberate focus. This is something that Sara Rees has consciously adopted.

"I'm naturally and have worked on myself to become, really positive and solutions-focussed in all of the relationships that I have. I think about the energy I bring to the relationship; I think about how I want people to feel when they see it's me ringing them, or my name on a list of meeting attendees or on something they'll be working with me on. I want them to feel that they would look forward to that and feel positively towards it."

Deliberately cultivating a positive energy that you take with you will help you to be memorable for the right reasons as you're focusing on how you want others to feel in your presence. Whether you're bright, bubbly and outgoing, or more thoughtful and quiet, you can still be memorable by the quality of how you show up and how you're being – it makes a huge difference.

Do Something Memorable

Once you know enough about people's values and preferences, and you've decided how you'd like people to experience you, then, of course the most obvious thing in being memorable is to do or say something worth remembering!

Nicky Ness shares a fabulous story. The powers that be decided to close the radio station that she worked in, and she decided she was not going to let that happen.

"I found a way to keep the station open. It was about using

my knowledge of how the MOD worked in Gibraltar, who the decision makers were here at HQ in the UK, knowing where the non-public money was and coming up with a plan that would pull all of those things together to keep the station open and that's what I did. That's part of the legacy that people still talk about now."

Now you may not have such huge plans or the scope in your current role for taking such big action - but do take some time to think about what you're currently working on, and consider how much impact you're making. Are you showcasing your skills to their best advantage? On a scale of 1 - 10, how committed are you to what you're doing and how much effort are you putting in? How could you inject some fresh energy and an invigorated approach to what you're doing regarding raising your profile? Are you thinking creatively about how you can achieve your work goals?

Another way to do this is to think again about the reputation you're busy creating for yourself and understand how you can enhance that, by becoming seen as an expert in your field. We'll talk about using social media in another chapter, but it's a great tool for helping you to be seen as a thought-leader. It's something that Carol Rosati has done, and she acknowledges that it takes time.

"I've seen how different recruitment is now and how you need to engage with social media and develop your profile, for example on LinkedIn. It's crucial if a woman wants to succeed in today's working society; they must become memorable and become an expert in their field. It's taken me seven years with Inspire, and now my profile is out there, and people know who I am. It's little steps - there's nothing 'one step' about this at all."

How can you begin to demonstrate your expertise a little more? And if you don't particularly feel much like an expert, then what can you do to keep up to date more in your subject area? Being able to discuss current industry issues and hot topics will showcase your knowledge and certainly help you to be remembered as someone who has their finger on the pulse of current thinking.

Try this: decide what you want to be known for and then think about how you can begin to achieve that. What do you want people to say about you? How can you deliberately and intentionally begin to make sure that you show up as that person – and be remembered the way you want to be remembered?

Be Authentic

Amanda Robinson, Head of Sales for Virgin Trains, agrees that it's important to be memorable – but what's more important is to be authentic.

"Being memorable is incredibly important, but don't be memorable for the wrong reasons, it's got to be real. I speak my mind, that's important to me. I have integrity, and I'm not a 'yes' person; they're my values. They are memorable because not everyone will be like that."

One of the common problems my clients bring to the table is that of learning to be themselves in a new role. They may have been recently promoted or made a career move that demands more of them, maybe leading staff or a team for the first time. In addition to the steep learning curve required in these situations, is the need to establish themselves as an authentic presence.

The problem is, in a new role, with new demands being made on you, who is the authentic you?

Jackie Daniel sums this up wonderfully.

"Early on in my career, I tried not to be memorable! I think it was fear – I wanted to look like the others. There's something interesting about my first board-level post; it was full of men, and I played down my female characteristics and traits, and I tried to blend in because that's what I thought success looked like. Now of course I try and stand out and absolutely know you can if you do it in the right way. I wear what I like instead of what I think I should wear, I wear my hair the way I want to, and I wear outlandish glasses. Whether you're talking or expressing an opinion, it's about being comfortable and authentic – that will make you memorable."

One definition of authenticity is to be genuine; it's the meaning most of my clients talk about when discussing the notion with me. They say things like 'This isn't who I am...' or 'It feels like an act, I'm just pretending...'. New challenges that come with new ways of being at work can feel uncomfortable.

This is why it's so tricky to talk about being authentic. Being authentic doesn't mean staying the same and never changing. It's a mistake to think we must be the same person in every situation and bear our souls and share every detail of who we are with work colleagues.

Discussing your latest argument with your spouse, turning the air blue with the habitual bad language we use with friends or sharing the details of your overdraft may be the 'authentic' you in one sense – but surely there's a time and a place for sharing those details or that side of you?

It's important to note that both Amanda and Jackie have a good understanding of their values, and it's those that shine through, along with *having confidence to be themselves in that particular role.*

Holding onto firm beliefs about what it means to be authentic can lead us to write rigid scripts about who we are and how we should behave. Change often causes problems, for others and often for ourselves if we don't understand that as humans we are constantly evolving and developing. The person we are today is not the person we were yesterday, and the person I am with my partner, parents and close friends may not be the person I am with colleagues.

How can we develop a useful definition of what it means to be authentic in a changing world?

Firstly, by understanding that we are many things to many people. In the Hindu faith, there is the notion of one god, many forms. And we are one human, many forms. I am Sue, the mother; Sue the writer; Sue the educator; Sue the wife. I am also Sue the impatient; Sue the procrastinator; Sue the amateur cook and wine lover. *Being authentic doesn't mean showing all of you, to all your colleagues, all the time.*

It's ok to be different things to different people and in different situations. We can decide who we need to be in the role we're in, become that person and become authentic in that.

Secondly, by considering what you don't know about yourself yet. We all have huge reserves of untapped potential –what we don't know about ourselves. Sometimes we can seem so certain about the future, our role in it and how we think we would respond to events and triggers, that we forget none of us has a crystal ball. All we can say for certain is that 'this is how I was in the past'. It's not necessarily an indication of what *will* happen. It is possible to learn new ways of responding and behaving – and when you do so, you're no less authentic for that. Our capacity for change is infinite and exciting and only stifled by our limiting thoughts.

Just because others may not have seen your skills, talents and ambitions yet, doesn't mean you don't have them. Remember that.

Lastly, understand that you are not the same person today that you were yesterday, or the day or year or decade before. Remember your first job? Just think about the skills you've learned since then, the experiences you've had and the knowledge you now have. You've changed, developed and grown since then. And your next new role will require you to change, grow and develop again.

Authenticity is about understanding who you are in the moment and knowing that we are complex creatures with different layers. We're not one-dimensional.

Herminia Ibarra discusses the fascinating topic of identity in *The Authenticity Paradox, HBR 2015.*

"Your leadership identity can and should change each time you move on to bigger and better things."

Understanding and accepting who you are, all of you, and expecting to change, can help you to be more comfortable with the different demands placed on you.

Try this: consider the many different roles you adopt in your life. How differently do you show up in each of them? Arriving at an understanding of your values can help you to drill down into the core of who you are, and you may find those stay the same, even though you may behave differently in different situations. Try the values exercise below to identify your current core values.

Values Exercise

These will help you to develop a clearer sense of what's important in your life and help you to build self-awareness and authenticity. Our values form the basis of who we are as a person, whether we are consciously aware of them or not.

In a business setting, it's important that your values match those of the industry in which you work.

"...when the values of the organisation are in alignment with the aspirational values of employees; the result is high performance. There is a high level of staff engagement and a pursuit of excellence regarding the quality of products and service."

Richard Barrett, The Barret Values Centre

Look at the list of values below, and you will find that lots of them will have no significance for you and that there will be a few that jump out at you.

The list is not exhaustive, and you may find there are other values important to you that are not listed here.

Acceptance; Accountability; Accuracy; Achievement; Adaptability; Adventure; Autonomy; Balance; Boldness; Calmness; Commitment; Cooperation; Control; Courage; Curiosity; Democracy; Detachment; Determination; Directness; Discipline; Economic security; Education; Effort; Empowerment; Enthusiasm; Equality; Excellence; Fairness; Family; Forgiveness; Freedom; Fun; Generosity; Gentleness; Happiness; Harmony; Health; Helpfulness; Honesty; Humility; Independence; Individualism; Integrity; Intuition; Joy; Justice; Kindness; Learning; Love; Loyalty; Mercy; Moderation; Modesty; Openness; Optimism; Patience; Peace; Perfection; Perseverance; Pleasure; Power; Prudence; Quality; Recognition; Respect; Responsibility; Risk-taking; Self-awareness; Sharing; Stability; Spirituality; Success; Tenacity; Thoughtfulness; Tolerance; Tradition; Trust; Truthfulness; Understanding; Variety; Vitality; Wealth; Wisdom; Warmth; Winning; Zeal; Wilfulness; Wonder

Next Steps

Consider each value in turn briefly, and pick one value that you feel you couldn't live without, and write it down.

Another way to do this is to think about the phrase that often gets uttered, "I hate it when..." The part in the dots, when turned on its head, will often turn out to be a core value for us. For example, I hate it when people are rude; courtesy and good manners matter to me (I value courtesy), and I strive to live this value in my daily life.

What would each value you have picked mean for you?

How do you know it's a value that's important to you?

Write a short description of how you interpret that value; two people with the same values may describe them in different ways.

How do you demonstrate that value at work? If I observed

you for a week, how would I see it in action?

Continue in this way, picking different values, until you have a list of between 5 and 10 values that resonate with you.

Chapter 8

Speak Up

"If you're not speaking up, then why are you around the table? If I'm halfway through a meeting and I haven't said anything, I ask myself what value am I adding here?"
Charlotte Sweeney, OBE, Inclusion Expert, Author and Founder of Charlotte Sweeney Associates

On the face of it, this is a simple strategy – yes, open your mouth and say something. And yet, it is a regular topic of discussion in my client's work, with women at all levels in organisations. I've worked with talented senior women who still feel intimidated at the boardroom table. The reality of being told to 'speak up' is that it's not as easy as we'd like to think, and yet if we don't do it, we can kiss our career goodbye.

In a series of articles in The New York Times in January 2015, *Speaking While Female; Why Women Stay Quiet at Work*, Sheryl Sandberg and Adam Grant highlighted examples of gender bias they attributed to some women's reluctance to speak up at work. There are well-documented reasons why some women stay silent.

"We've both seen it happen again and again. When a woman speaks in a professional setting, she walks a tightrope. Either she's barely heard, or she's judged as too aggressive. When a man says virtually the same thing, heads nod in appreciation for his fine idea. As a result, women often decide that saying less is more."

Again, I've met with similar tales from clients; unconscious gender bias is widespread, and we need to find a way to tackle it. The articles are an excellent read with some useful ideas, so I'd certainly recommend you take a look at them. They highlight one of the main challenges women face, but it's by no means the only one.

Heather Melville shared a story with me...

"I once sat in a meeting where I was the only woman. Every time I opened my mouth to say something, the men all talked over me. So, I stood up, and they all thought I was going to the bathroom. It wasn't until I banged the glass water bottle with my pen that they all looked and I said 'Now I've got your attention, I'd like to say...' They were all shocked because they didn't recognise their behaviour or the impact it had on me."

If you want to move your career forward, then learning to be bold and speaking up is a must. It's something you can't avoid, despite how challenging it might feel at times. If you want to lead, then you'll need to get comfortable with speaking up, even in situations where it's a real effort to physically get your voice heard. Working on your mindset and confidence levels will help here. A little self-belief goes a long way, as does some tenacity. Heather's example here is bold, quite frankly brilliant and direct. You may not feel ready for this kind of move yet, but there are lots of ways you can learn to exercise the 'speak up' muscle, and in doing so, raise your profile and visibility.

This chapter contains ideas to help you develop your ability to speak up in a range of settings and situations so that you can build your reputation as someone with valuable ideas and opinions.

And if ever you're in doubt about your ability to share valuable ideas and hold pertinent opinions, then here's what Nicky Hill, Director of HR at Nottingham University Hospitals NHS Trust has to say:

"Go and ask someone who knows you well and ask them how often you say something that's complete nonsense. You'll find that it's pretty rare."

If you're sitting there worrying about making a daft point, remember that feedback you've been given and speak up.

Here's how.

Make Small Talk

Whenever I tell clients to try this, it gets a mixed response. I've had some workshop attendees dismiss it out of hand, and others sneer at me. But honestly, if you can't initiate and maintain a conversation with someone on a one-to-one level, then how on earth are you going to build strong enough relationships, so you can have the more meaningful conversations with the people that can help you to build your career?

If you want to further your career in any way, then surely the ability to talk to other people, from all levels of seniority, in a range of settings, is an absolute pre-requisite for success?

Beverley Smith told me this is something that she's always done throughout her career; knowing a bit about the people she was working with has been crucial to her understanding of things that may influence how they work and how you deal with them. And it's something that worked wonders for her career too.

"I've always done this. When I was a planning enforcement officer, I built a relationship with my first chief executive. I'd say hello to her in the corridor, and that small talk made sure I was not just some unnamed person at work. She was the one who gave me my first career boost."

The ability to engage others in conversation, put them at ease and help them to feel accepted is a real skill and people who have this talent are engaging, charismatic and unforgettable.

How you leave people feeling in business and life really matters. If you are someone who shows no interest in the person in front of you, or you are unresponsive and difficult to get a word out of, then I'd argue that your relationships will suffer, and your visibility and profile on the back of it.

This is something that Jane Scott Paul agrees with. "Small talk is very important, but people just don't get it. I've had to go to some of the most excruciatingly dull dinners over the years. My friend and I would have bets about how many times we would be asked an open question - you'd had a good evening if you'd been asked two! There's always something interesting about people even if they don't seem promising at first!"

Many years ago, I was in New York, as a guest at a business dinner. The chap sitting next to me answered all of my questions in mono-syllables and made no effort to develop the conversation. In the end, I asked him what he did when he wasn't sitting having dinner at the club we were at – and told him to make it up if he wanted to, I wouldn't mind. He looked suitably shame-faced at this point and did make more of an effort for the rest of the dinner – but I've never forgotten how I felt, trying to talk to someone who had no interest in me.

Most conversations are started with some form of 'chat' first, to break the ice, find common ground and build some ease and trust. We look for things in common, beyond the work agenda – that's where relationships are built.

This can also help you if you're feeling intimidated and nervous in a situation that you might feel out of your depth in. First time in a senior management meeting? Knowing that the other person has a mortgage, teenagers or elderly parents to look after, enjoys cooking programmes and likes to cycle at the weekend can help you to see them as more human, rather than the nerve-inducing distant figure they may seem. Simply arriving early and chatting over a coffee could be a way to engage new colleagues and de-mystify them!

You don't have to be an extrovert to do this either; introverts can make small talk too. Whatever situation you're in, focus on building relationships one person at a time. It's about showing an interest in someone else.

Try this: how can you build relationships with those people you meet? Know what's going on in the world and have something to say about some of it. Develop some interests outside of work that makes you an interesting person to talk to. Practice your open questioning skills so you can start and maintain a conversation with anyone you meet.

Change your Mindset

One way to feel more comfortable about speaking up is by understanding that it doesn't always have to be about you. You can raise your profile by sharing the love of others. This is a great way to demonstrate the success that your team has had working with you, showcasing their achievements and how you've empowered them to achieve great things. It will also help them to feel amazing about their achievements too.

Many years ago, I was the press officer at the school I worked in. I managed to get us into the local papers on a weekly basis – this was pre-internet. It meant the school got great publicity, the children and parents liked to see us being featured and the staff felt that their work was getting noticed by a wider audience. It also meant that when the paper was looking for an angle for a story, we were their first choice, every time.

On a personal basis, it raised my profile with the governors hugely. This came in useful when I applied to go on an exchange to New York City for four weeks – they knew who I was and associated the school's high profile locally with me, which worked in my favour and I was given permission to go. They also made a point of thanking me personally for all my contribution to the school's success.

I'd not shared anything about myself except a few occasions when my class were featured – I'd talked solely about the work of the wider school.

Before my trip, the paper covered a story about me taking part in the exchange, which again raised the profile of the school in the local business community who had organised the trip. A win-win for everyone concerned.

This is an approach that Jo Cox-Brown has used in the past.

"Sharing what you've learned is celebrating with your team. People would say 'oh you're always in the papers' and I would say that I'm sharing excellence, and I'm sharing it with the world. I'm just sharing the journey – I think it's important not to be afraid to do that. It really helps the team; they can say that we were on Songs of Praise, or on the BBC or in the Independent. It's a thing they can feel pride and excitement in."

You can be visible and take others with you on that journey.

Try this: if sharing your achievements feels a little challenging to begin with, identify what you've done as a team recently that you could share. Consider how you could do this to a wider audience of your peers, colleagues and clients. How can you find ways to do this consistently?

Speak to Your Boss

Your immediate boss is someone who can help you to further your career, so it's important that you're able to speak to them. Hopefully, you've got a relationship with them that is good, and they are fairly approachable. This is an approach that can feel challenging, especially if you are inexperienced – but you'll need to bite the bullet and get used to speaking to more senior staff.

Jackie Daniel acknowledges that this might be hard to do when you lack courage in the early part of your career. "I can see how I've shifted as I've got older and wiser. It's so important to do it. With my staff now, I want to hear their comments. I love people who come and knock on my door and insist I hear their ideas. Nine times out of ten, they're fantastic, and I'm really glad I did."

Your boss will also have a different perspective and a broader view of some of the issues involved in furthering your career. They will also know about a range of opportunities and will have a wider, deeper network at a more senior level that they will be able to help you access.

When I first started networking, one of the Directors of the organisation came to a meeting. Afterwards, we held a meet and greet with him – except no one spoke to him! Seeing him sitting alone, I went across and started talking to him. He remarked at how no one else had the courage to approach him and what a shame that was. I was able to ask his advice about building my network and got 20 minutes of his undivided attention.

Sometimes more senior staff can feel quite isolated and apart from the rest of their staff, especially in larger organisations – and more junior staff often feel in awe of them too. You'll stand out by being bold enough to speak to them.

A past client told me about a male colleague who regularly made appointments with the Vice Chancellor of the University they worked in. She had no idea what about but watched as their relationship deepened. Working on helping my client overcome a mindset that told her she couldn't do that, gave her a valuable tool. If you have something to say, then why not approach more senior staff?

Carolyn Pearson puts the need for this approach beautifully bluntly; "Speak to your boss. Even if you think your boss is an idiot, they'll need some love and attention from you! To get on that next rung up the ladder, you have to make your boss feel like you've got their back. If your boss is a liability, there's a fine line between distancing yourself and you still helping them to feel ok, and distancing yourself through silly and inappropriate body language in meetings, like eye raising and so on."

Try this: make sure that you cultivate a good relationship with your boss. Get to know them as a person and don't be afraid to say hello when you see them. Understand their priorities and values and make sure that you affirm those rather than offend them. Get good at 'managing up' – this is about being conscious of your boss's objectives and working towards helping him or her achieve them.

It's about understanding your boss and knowing how best to communicate with them, their likes and dislikes, what makes them tick and how you can get the best out of your relationship with them. If your relationship isn't in good shape, then you'll need to consider what's getting in the way, and what you're prepared to do about it.

Remember, you also have more senior leaders; you can also begin to cultivate relationships with them, making sure that you're doing so in a way that won't make an already rocky relationship with your immediate boss, any worse.

Speaking to your boss makes it much easier to do this...

Let Your Ambitions be Known

The more I work with clients and run workshops, the more I'm convinced that this is a huge part of being successful. The truth is, if no one knows what your ambitions are, then you're unlikely to be considered for the kinds of roles you're looking for – and you'll be missing out on a whole heap of support that could come your way in helping you to get that next role.

A client on a workshop of mine many years ago had a penny-dropping moment in just this way. As we were working on ways to become more visible, she suddenly realised that the new role her manager was talking about, was one she wanted herself. She emailed me very excitedly a week later to tell me that she'd gone back to work and asked the question 'What about me?'

The result?

Her first leadership role, with the terms and conditions of the position adjusted to suit her circumstances.

Tiffany Hall agrees.

"We underestimate the extent to which stating a preference for something can make it happen. The number of times that conversation 'I'd be interested in doing this' or 'I'd really like to grow this part of my experience' will fall at times of serendipity or luck is surprising and surprisingly frequent."

It's easy to be forgotten if you don't keep your leader or manager up to date with what your ambitions are and what you're prepared to do. People are masters of assumption – if you don't tell them what you want, they'll be making it up for you, and it may not work in your favour.

If you are willing to travel, study, take on extra projects or develop your career in a particular direction, then the people with the power to make those decisions and help you move onwards and upwards will need to know. Caroline Welch-Ballentine agrees. "I can see this in HR; people get forgotten if they don't make a little bit of noise. We do occasionally have to say, 'I'm here, this is what I want'. Maybe the company can't give it to you at that time – but at least if the discussion is out there, it's clear that you want something."

Now I'm not saying that it's necessarily a good thing to march into your boss's office and tell them that you want their job! But, indicating that you're open to learning and any opportunities that come your way, and letting them know that you feel you have more to offer the organisation, are ways to signal that you're ambitious.

Asking for, or attending training and development opportunities fall into this category too. Signalling that you're a lifelong learner tells others that you're committed to your career and development. It's great if your organisation will fund your CPD – but if they won't, then do think about investing in yourself. And find a way to make sure that they know this!

Don't expect to be fed opportunities on a plate – it doesn't work like that. Simply expecting others to notice what you're good at and then waiting for them to approach you with your dream role will rarely happen. Don't risk being overlooked – ask for what you want.

Being bold can work. It's an approach that Kate Roebuck, Partner at Bridge McFarland Solicitors, took in her career when she joined the law firm. "I said, I'd like to join you as a partner; I'm fine with joining as a salaried partner, but if we like each other, I want an equity partnership at the end of the year."

And that's just what she got.

Try this: know your worth and have a conversation. Pick your time and place and let your boss know everything you're prepared to do. Ask some questions. What do you need to do to take the next step up in your organisation or industry? What experience would they be looking for? What would they recommend? What did they do to get to where they are? What tips do they have to offer you? What's the best route to get to where you want to go?

Whenever you encounter more senior colleagues, ask them the same questions. You'd be pleasantly surprised at how open people are to this line of enquiry. Have one question up your sleeve and ask it whenever you get the chance – maybe something along the lines of 'What one piece of advice would you give to an ambitious ... if they were serious about getting to ... in this organisation/industry.' You'll be signalling your intent, as well as subtly affirming their own position.

Chapter 9

Have an Advocate Speak Up for You

"I had my children... and I do wonder whether I'd still be practising if I didn't have two great supporters. Strong and supportive coaches, mentors, a champion, an advocate – if you're moving up the chain, you need to have a champion who will put your name forward for opportunities."
Karen Friebe, Partner at Berwin Leighton Paisner

Learning to speak up for ourselves is something we should all do, and it's a skill that we need in abundance.

There is, however, an undeniable strength in the social proof of someone else singing our praises. Customer feedback, satisfaction surveys, 9 out of 10 cats, these kinds of phrases are bandied around freely in the advertising world. If you can find someone who will speak up for you and promote you when opportunities arise, then you'll notice the difference in your career.

You may already have a mentor, someone who you can speak to about different aspects of your work, who knows where you're coming from and where you're likely to be heading and has the experience to help guide your journey.

An advocate, sponsor or champion, however, is someone who will speak *about you*. It's like having an ally – a personal spokesperson who will use their position, contacts and connections at a much more senior level to open doors for you that might otherwise remain closed. They are generally someone far more senior to yourself and can be tricky to find. You're talking about someone who is willing to put their reputation on the line when it comes to recommending you, so this isn't an overnight or easy option. And it's one that is underused by women.

As Kate Turner says, "If you can achieve this, it's amazing for your career. It is hard to achieve in work, but you do find that people who have sponsors get much further on."

An article in Forbes, by Sylvia Ann Hewlett, *Find a Sponsor Instead of a Mentor* (September 2013), supports this.

"...70% of sponsored men and 68% of sponsored women feel they are progressing through the ranks at a satisfactory pace, compared to 57% of their unsponsored peers."

Advocacy, or sponsorship of women, seems to be a challenge and not yet commonplace. Only two of the women I interviewed had direct experience of having an advocate, even though the majority could see the benefits of this approach clearly.

So, just how do you go about finding yourself an advocate, champion or sponsor?

How to Find an Advocate

Be Visible

Ironically, one way to attract an advocate is by being good at the very subject matter of this book! Just to remind you, you'll never experience the career success you want while you're the best-kept secret in your organisation, and the same goes for having a sponsor.

Your more senior colleagues need to know who are you and what you can do and, as busy people, you'll need to make this as easy for them as possible.

A particularly impressive example of this presented itself to me some years ago, as I was delivering some training to the UK HQ of a global organisation. In the room were the top UK 'movers and shakers', along with the UK head of sales. There was also a woman who wasn't any of the above. It turns out that she was there because of a great piece of profile-raising which still impresses me to this day.

She'd spotted a flaw in an internal operating procedure and had developed an approach to overcome it. After writing a white paper about it, she approached the UK head of sales and shared her findings with him. The rest is history. She was in the room that day being groomed for a job several steps above her current position.

Advocacy works if you can be visible enough – and good enough at what you do too. If her idea was bad, or her reputation wasn't robust enough in the first place, I dare say she wouldn't have been there, so really there's a bit of a holy trinity going on here. Visibility – Reputation – Performance. A powerful combination.

Try this: make sure that your reputation and performance will survive the scrutiny of more senior staff and that you're doing enough to be seen by them. This is a time when being great at what you do really does matter; your results need to be impressive, and your reputation needs to work well for you. Remember the advice in the last chapter too – at some point, you will need to make your ambitions known.

Plan Ahead and Connect

If you haven't used the career planning tool in Chapter One, then do give it a go. It makes it very difficult to know who you need to connect to if you don't know where you're going and whose orbit you'll need to be in. Make sure that you understand who the influential people are, know who is well connected, and crucially, the colleagues/connections that are going places themselves. Research the reputations of more senior staff to make sure that you're not throwing your lot in with someone who has no more clout than yourself. This may sound calculated – I prefer to use the word strategic.

And why restrict yourself to one advocate?

As Jayne Mitchell says, "I've never deliberately used an

advocate, but I do know they can be incredibly helpful and powerful. Knowing that you have some people who are influential and can talk about you maintains your confidence, and you'll know which people to go to for support on particular issues. Your visibility and contributions will be different in different settings, so knowing who to pick is quite important. For example, people I know have seen me operate in different ways, be it nationally or internationally, so I can approach a variety of people who can speak about different aspects of my work."

Find the right networks of senior staff and connect widely with them, building rapport and relationships. Remember, finding an advocate takes time.

This is an approach I helped one of my clients develop. Keen to be considered for an internal promotion, she set about assessing the potential impact of senior staff to advocate and support her within her organisation and then categorised them accordingly. She came up with a list of those who were the most influential and from there developed a plan to connect with them and nurture those relationships as a way of having a layer of advocacy at a level or two higher in seniority to her boss. The tool we came up with (The IIDA Grid) is at the end of this chapter.

Try this: if you haven't already, use the career planning tool. Then look at your networks. You're looking for allies and influencers to begin building connections with. Influencers are people with power whose voice gets heard; allies are those who share your views, understand the value that you add, see your capabilities, trust you to deliver to a high standard and support you. A combination of both qualities in one person would make a great advocate or sponsor. Use the IIDA grid below to help you sort through your connections.

The IIDA Grid

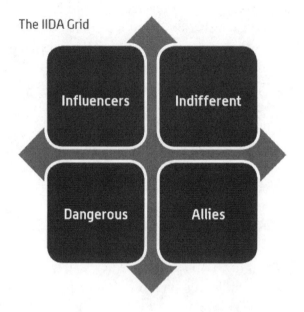

Take some time to consider your organisation, department or industry and think about the following types of people in relation to your own ambitions and where they might fit into this grid.

Influencers

These are people with power – their voice gets heard, and their opinions hold sway, and they have their finger on the pulse of current events. They carry an authority with them that doesn't always necessarily come with their position, but they are a force to be reckoned with in a positive way. They have the potential to support you.

Indifferent

These are people who simply turn up and do their job. They are not involved in the internal politics of the organisation and don't want to be. They are impervious to what goes on around them provided they can get on with their job, and nothing affects them too directly and present no threat to your own goals.

Dangerous

These are people who may have a keen eye for what is going on and may share your aspirations or have another agenda for ensuring that you are not successful. In this way, they may be someone who represents a danger to your personal goals and ambitions.

Allies

These are people who share your views and support you. They are people who can be relied upon to advance your cause, posing no active threat.

Some Questions to Consider:

1. How connected to the Influencers are you, and how can you deepen those relationships to begin to build alliances with them?
2. How can you minimise the threat of the Dangerous? What do you need to know about them?
3. How could you begin to build relationships with the Indifferent to create Allies to widen your support?
4. How can you build new Allies at a more senior level to ensure you have appropriate support?
5. How much of an Influencer are you seen as, and what do you need to do to be seen as more of one in your own right?

The answers to these questions will help you to form an action plan and be more strategic about how you are perceived and positioned – and how to identify potential advocates.

Chapter 10

Become Known in your Wider Industry

"I made a deliberate decision at one point in my career, based on where I felt I could get different sets of experiences and networks, connections and visibility, both within the University sector and at the same time build a national and international profile. As a result, my network is so much more extensive, and I am known by the national bodies that are important to every institution."
Professor Jayne Mitchell, Deputy Vice-Chancellor, Bishop Grosseteste University

At the beginning of your career, you may be chasing an internal promotion as your first step up the career ladder. To do that, you'll need to be well-networked internally, so this strategy may seem like something you'll need to do 'one day' – or may just feel like a step too far in terms of visibility.

However, there are huge benefits to be had from widening your 'platform' and becoming more visible in this way. Once you know where you're going and what you want to be known for, you can set about building your reputation in that area. Jayne Mitchell clearly demonstrates how being strategic has worked for her. You can begin to do the same.

This means that when the time is right, you'll be a credible commentator or thought leader in your field, with a wide network – and you'll be perfectly positioned to move into more senior roles.

Charlotte Sweeney sums up the need to do this very nicely:

"It elevates you from an 'internal' person with knowledge to an industry expert."

It's essential if you're looking to move into different organisations, and often takes a certain degree of courage to begin promoting yourself in this way, especially at first. You may need to begin showcasing yourself before you feel ready for it and it can feel very uncomfortable, depending on what you choose to do – but go with it. There are lots of different ways to do this, which we'll get to in a moment.

The other point to note here is that it often takes time too. Carol Rosati told me that it's taken seven years for her to build her profile and become a recognisable name in her field. This is why it's not a wise move to wait to begin to do this – it's a slow build, years rather than months. A little planning ahead can help you to be strategic about this and if you haven't looked at the chapter on career-planning then why not pop back and give it a go. The results will help you to think carefully about how to make the most of this strategy.

Apart from positioning yourself as an industry expert, a wider public profile can also mean a wider support network for the times when things may get challenging, as Fiona Cownie points out, "… you'll have a network of friends and colleagues who aren't affected by what's going on at work, and they can be very supportive when things go wrong. It helps give you some self-confidence."

Being more widely known gives you more choices and more flexibility over what you choose to do. When you feel that you have more choices, you're less likely to feel hemmed in by potentially stressful current circumstances, and this can free you up to make bolder moves career-wise. Why stay somewhere you're unhappy if you know there's a different world out there, with amazing opportunities just waiting to be seized?

A wider platform also means a wider awareness of exactly what's out there and what new possibilities exist, for you to seize those chances.

There's also a huge benefit to your organisation in being

more widely known. Nicky Ness says "I'm well known in the radio industry in the UK. I'm part of the Radio Academy, the UK Radio Skills Council and I'm on the organising committee for our big conference. I've been able to do lots of deals for BFBS as a result of this."

So what tools and approaches are there for becoming more widely known in your industry? In this chapter, let's talk about social media.

Social Media

The power of this cannot be underestimated; understand where your sector and industry contacts are and make sure you're there too. Be aware that things can move quickly, and groups of professionals can spring up in places you wouldn't expect.

For example, when I first returned to the UK after working overseas, I found a handful of schools on Twitter. Seven years on, there is a huge community of teachers, senior leaders and educators engaging on Twitter, exchanging best practice, debating pedagogy, supporting each other and promoting the advancement of women leaders in education. It's a vibrant and vocal community that is also super-active off social media too, with regular meet-ups as part of the #womened movement.

You'll need to find out where your 'crowd' are online. If the key influencers in your industry hang out on Twitter, then you ought to think about it too.

Twitter

Twitter is my favourite, which I credit with helping me to be where I am today. When I returned from Central America, I set myself up a Twitter account and began following local people in the hope that they would follow me back. Most of them did. I built relationships with them and soon learned about offline networking meetings too and went along to a few.

Twitter is a platform where you can contact just about

anyone, and you have a strong chance of them responding to you. I've found that it levels the playing field – yes, some people are not going to reply to you, but over time, if you aim at building relationships and interact with others in a respectful and intelligent way, then I think it's possible to get yourself on the radar of some influential people. This is one the reasons I like Twitter – people are less precious about themselves, than they are, say on LinkedIn.

I credit Twitter with raising my profile and the ways it has made that possible include:

- Connecting me with the BBC – I said 'yes' to my first BBC interview after being messaged by a BBC Radio reporter. This has led to regular appearances on BBC Radio as well as paid work with them
- Finding my own mentors and coaches
- Being given guest blogging opportunities
- Being given introductions to podcast interviewers
- Providing a platform for selling my first book
- Providing a platform for readership of my articles and blog posts
- Providing a showcase for my skills which has led to client work
- Being asked to speak at events
- Being asked to take part in Twitter chats as an 'expert'
- Finding CPD opportunities
- Learning new skills and approaches which I transfer into my work, which keeps me up to date and visible
- Connecting with industry experts
- Receiving praise and thanks for my work in a public forum
- Being able to answer questions to demonstrate expertise

The list could go on.

Some women I talk to shy away from social media because

they see it as being too time-consuming, particularly Twitter, or else they don't understand how it works. Or, you may already be using social media socially and haven't given any thought to how you could use it to raise your profile and help you to be more visible.

It can become a bottomless time-pit, it's true, so it's up to you to manage yourself appropriately and ensure you set yourself strong boundaries. With a little discipline, it can become a fabulous place for learning and connection, raising your profile in the process; it's worth taking the time to get to grips with it.

Heather Melville understands the power of social media, "We've built a big following in the Women's Network, and we tweet about women and clients. It's absolutely key."

Likewise, Charlotte Sweeney increasingly uses it, adding, "I'm very clear on what my message is – so on any social media out there about me, it's always very professional and consistent."

She makes a pertinent point here – social media is a powerful force and can damage your reputation as much as it can build it. Be careful about what you post, and the message you're giving out. Decide what you would like to be known for and then ensure that everything you post consistently supports that message.

Make sure on all the social media accounts that you're going to use professionally, that you have a suitable profile picture that reflects your message and how you want to be perceived.

Let's look at Twitter – how can you get started?

1. The simplest and easiest way to start is just to follow some people in your industry and reply to their tweets. Hang out on the Twitter platform for a few hours and watch what happens and then join in by answering a tweet, or by retweeting (sharing) something someone has tweeted. The chances are they'll thank you, and then you can begin to strike up a conversation – or else ask them a question about something they've tweeted. This

is a great way of getting to very influential people and having them notice you – if you persevere and tweet relevant, interesting and thoughtful comments, in time, they may engage with you.

2. Share your content as you produce it – and if you aren't producing any yet, then that will need to change. There is a huge opportunity to build your network further and contact the movers and shakers in your industry, by commenting on and sharing their work too. Jackie Daniel is also a big fan of Twitter, "I've had to learn how to use it, and learn about writing blogs, so I'm not just writing three lines but attaching something of value." I think she makes a strong point here – it's not all about sharing picture quotes and what you've had for your dinner, although a few personal updates are a good thing.

3. Your use of Twitter is about showcasing yourself and sharing your expertise as a professional. Make sure that you add value. If necessary, keep a personal Twitter account separate from a professional one; several of the women I interviewed did this. Pictures of you falling down drunk at the weekend probably won't impress the right people – and social media has a long, unforgiving history.

4. Try joining Twitter chats/debates that are hashtagged – a hashtag is a way of pulling together all the comments and updates on a single topic. For example, #SLTChat is a weekly twitter chat about senior leadership in education, where teachers, head teachers and other thought leaders contribute to various discussions on the future of education.

5. You can also follow industry magazines and publications and comment on articles they publish and respond to calls for guest contributors. I've had considerable success myself with this, and have grown my following and engagement after guest blogging for someone very well respected in the leadership world.

6. When I started using Twitter, I put together a spreadsheet. It contained tips for professionals who might follow me; links to articles and blogs I'd written; links to articles other people had written; some relevant quotes; links to relevant YouTube videos; book recommendations and questions about pertinent topics. It gave me subjects to tweet about as I was building up connections, and it could be a good starting point for you if you're completely new to Twitter, simply do a search for relevant hashtags to include with each tweet, and you'll be away.

7. Find others to follow by looking at the followers of people you're already connected to – this means you'll be building up a network of people interested in similar subjects to yourself and quite possibly your industry. It will raise your visibility amongst them, and you can begin building up relationships with them.

8. Post regularly and consistently and you'll soon begin to build up a following and have an audience for your posts.

What else is there to use?

LinkedIn and Facebook are two other popular social media platforms where you can begin to build your platform, be more visible and get your voice heard.

LinkedIn

LinkedIn is a professional networking platform and a more formal online space, although there have been complaints recently about it becoming another Facebook, with members posting updates that are considered unprofessional. Remember – consider what you want to be known for and then ensure everything you post online reflects that.

Because there's not the restriction of 280 characters as with Twitter, there's more debate on posts, and as a result, you have a bigger space and opportunity to express your views.

On LinkedIn, you also have the option to post in groups, which is another area for you to show off your expertise by answering questions and sharing relevant articles, although often group owners don't like you to post your links. And of course, on LinkedIn, you can ask for recommendations and receive endorsements, which is a perfect way of showcasing your expertise.

There are plenty of books, articles and experts out there that will keep you up to date with how LinkedIn works and what you'll need to do to optimise your profile – if your industry key influencers are active on LinkedIn then you should be too. It's worth taking the time to set up your profile properly, and consistency and regularity are just as important as they are on Twitter.

For both of these social media sites, I'd recommend the use of an app called Flipboard, which lets you follow and collate articles into magazines, from which you can share useful, current content, across a range of media. It's extremely useful and a great way to keep yourself up to date by reading new content in one place. You can then share that content with a suitable comment (on Twitter) or commentary (on LinkedIn) and begin to demonstrate your expertise and invite engagement from your followers.

Facebook

Facebook can be a mixed bag. Unless you run your own business, the main reason for using it is likely to be personal. There are, however, some useful groups that you can find, which can be very supportive. One such group is Women Who Speak, a group that does what it says on the tin. At the time of writing, there are over 4,500 members, who have access to a rich source of experience and support in the speaking industry. The moderators and members are generous with their time and considerable expertise.

This has the effect of boosting your skills – which will raise your profile as you speak, and it gets you in front of another audience; you never know who may be in that group. I've been approached for speaking gigs after someone has clicked through onto my profile and seen what I do.

Posting updates about what you're doing – for example, attending a conference, or a picture of you giving a talk – on your personal page is also a good way of highlighting what you're up to.

I regularly share pictures of the journals I buy for a workshop I run – my Facebook friends now come to expect the photo when I run the day, and they all post what they think of them on my personal timeline. From this, I've had the opportunity of running the workshop internally for national organisations and charities, as people I'm connected to noticed what I was doing.

You never know who is watching – and I don't mean that in a creepy sense. Taking a few pictures of your conference badge, or your cup of tea on the train when you're travelling to the conference, or even the room you're working in, with the organisation's logo subtly in the background can be a good way to raise awareness of what you're doing without feeling like you're shouting it from the rooftops – although if you want to do that too, that's perfectly ok!

Try this: review your current use of social media. Understand where your current key influencers tend to congregate on social media, and then ensure that you are there too. Set up an account if you don't already have one and connect with key people in your industry. Watch how they interact; share some of their content, or ask questions about it. Find some industry-relevant articles and share them, asking a question about the comment. Make sure you respond to anyone who replies to you. Aim to connect with one new person a day.

Chapter 11

Use Writing and Speaking

"Become clear what you want to be known for. I now write thought pieces, start debates and speak at conferences – it opens all sorts of doors and gets you into spaces that you wouldn't have thought of."
Dame Jackie Daniel, NHS Chief Executive

Using public speaking and writing is a necessary step in raising your profile outside your organisation.

Some industries, like academia, require you to write and publish – it's how you're known and how your reputation and impact is built. As Fiona Cownie told me, "You need to identify the key things that are valued by the people that are going to promote you."

Karen Friebe makes a similar point about speaking. "I've recently asked a young woman lawyer who is up for promotion to partnership, to step up and present at a big conference. If you want to do this kind of work, you'll be able to say you've presented to 150 people at a conference – it will really help her."

Both speaking and writing can feel challenging. Jackie Daniel goes on to say that when she started doing them early on in her career, that she found it intensely uncomfortable. There are many statistics bandied around that tell us that people fear public speaking above dying, and for some people, the thought of putting their ideas into words for others to read, is a deal-breaker.

However, to be known in your wider industry, getting to grips with one or both, is a skill you need to hone.

In the previous chapter, we talked about using social media to engage with others in your network and further afield, by building relationships and sharing information.

Speaking at conferences and writing takes this one step further. Rather than relying on other people's content and opinions, you should begin to develop your own unique voice. Finding this voice by understanding your professional identity will help you to build a reputation for yourself. Decide what you want to be known for – what's your message? This is closely tied in with what you stand for, and what drives you to get out of bed in the morning and do your job.

Effective, memorable and charismatic leaders are driven to make a difference. What's yours?

Early on in your career this may be hard to answer, but as you develop, grow and gain more experience, this will unfold for you. A good place to start is simply knowing what you want other people to know and think about you – what impression do you want to create, and how are you going to set about achieving this?

How does your attitude, behaviour and mindset help you to make sure that the message you want others to take away from you matches the one they actually get? Are you consistently showing up as that person, or is your behaviour getting in the way?

The other thing to consider is your viewpoint and opinion on industry-related topics. How up to date are you with current thinking in various areas, and what is your take on those topics? Form an opinion and find some evidence to back it up.

Can you find a different angle or idea? Do you disagree? Why? What would your ideas look like? Do you hold controversial thoughts about certain topics?

All of these questions can help you to begin to develop a voice of growing authority in your field and will provide you with the substance you will need when it comes to writing and speaking.

A message, an opinion, and a platform for sharing those things will help you to become more widely known.

Let's start with writing.

Writing

You don't have to be JK Rowling to write. It's perfectly acceptable to start small and have a limited audience for your first pieces. As your writing develops, so will your own unique 'voice'. Over time this will strengthen, and you'll begin to embody this; it will become who you are, and how you show up.

Here are some ideas to get started:

1. Begin by posting updates on LinkedIn. This gives you a chance to formulate your ideas and gain confidence in sharing them. Read around your chosen topic and find a few examples to comment on, or hypothesise about. Write with authority. You'll soon find that your own opinions develop, as does your writing style, which means you'll be more willing to try longer pieces.

2. Contribute to an internal newsletter. Most of your colleagues who compile these are probably only too keen for contributions. Find out what topics they are currently looking for and set yourself the challenge of producing an article.

   This is something that Charlotte Sweeney did from early on in her career. "I had a very clear vision that I wanted to have my name in things like HR Magazine, and People Management, so I used newsletters to practice writing articles on a regular basis."

   Here, she demonstrates how important it is to have an idea of where you are going in your career, as well as developing your voice, and practising using it. Contributing to an internal newsletter will give you the confidence to begin expanding your writing.

3. Begin blogging. A blog is an online platform that contains articles written by yourself or other people. You can set

one up for free and use it to host your writing, publishing enough articles to keep your readers interested. As we've discussed before, consistency is important. You can pick your topic and aim for around 500 words as a minimum, but they don't need to be *War and Peace*. The content is easy to share on social media, which will help you to build up a following. It's possible to build a strong following quickly in this way and is an ideal way to raise your profile if you combine it with social media.

4. Guest blog. Once you've found your blogging voice, then a great way to boost your visibility is by writing for other bloggers. Hopefully, you will have built a list of influential people and thought leaders in your industry, as well as online magazines. Apart from creating their own content, a number of them will probably be looking for other people to write posts for them. Some will ask for original material, or others may want to share previously published work.

I regularly guest blog for a US leadership coach, Jo Miller, on the Women's Leadership Coaching blog, *Be Leaderly*. This has given me an international platform, which has driven book sales, introduced me to thought leaders in the area of women's leadership, and led to new clients.

Influential and respected blogging platforms/ online magazines can boost your visibility hugely – The Huffington Post, Inc. and Forbes are some well-known examples.

5. Write a white paper. This is a longer article, which discusses a specific issue in more depth, outlining the problems and suggesting solutions. It's a great way to grow your authority in a particular area and demonstrate

your expertise; Carolyn Pearson's opinion is that it's these that will attract academic attention, and that of news organisations, such as Forbes. She also goes on to say, "Your boss will think you're fabulous if you're putting in the discretionary effort into writing a white paper on top of everything else you're doing." Your white paper can be shared via your blog, or someone else's or given away to people you meet at networking events or conferences. It's a useful tool to have up your sleeve when you follow up after meeting someone new. As a way of helping you to develop your thinking at a deeper, more strategic level, it's an invaluable tool.

6. Write for industry magazines and journals. Once you've found your writing voice and have some credibility established, then you may well find that your industry will be keen to share your content.

7. Conduct some independent research. This can set you head and shoulders above others; having an original viewpoint and evidence to back it up will help you to be taken more seriously. Carolyn Pearson includes this approach in her professional toolkit. "I was recently asked to speak at a Keynote Duty of Care Conference, about the safety of workers traveling overseas. The audience were security experts and I was talking about women's issues when travelling. I knew I'd have to come up with something more than regurgitating what's already out there, so I ran some independent research which knocked the socks off the guys in the room."

8. Write a book. If writing turns out to be a talent of yours, and you have a message that you want to share, then consider writing your own book. The ability to self-

publish means producing a book is possible for us all. This does wonders for your credibility and will work to raise your profile. By this point, you may be considered an authority in your area.

Now let's look at speaking.

Speaking

Public speaking has the reputation of striking fear into the hearts of many, which causes a lot of people to dismiss this way of raising their profile. However, if you can develop the skills to do this well, it carries huge impact.

"Speaking at conferences is something I've really focused on over the last four years. It takes you out of your comfort zone but positions you as an expert in your industry by giving you the credibility you need to become established in a certain area." Sara Rees

If you're new to this, then I wouldn't recommend starting with a conference – as always, one step at a time. There's also a reason I talked about writing first; it gives you the chance to develop your ideas and work on creating an informed platform from which you can communicate. Once you have found your voice in your writing, it's much easier to get used to the sound of hearing your voice in front of others. You'll sound and feel more credible having thought out your approach to your topics of interest, and by now you'll have an opinion you'll want to share. It has to be said that nerves can floor the best of us – see my advice for developing a success routine at the end of this chapter.

Here are some speaking ideas to get you started:

1. Start by making sure that your voice gets heard in meetings. Set yourself the challenge of having something to say every time you're in one.

2. Get used to giving presentations. Again, these may make you feel uncomfortable, to begin with, but it's well worth honing your skills so that you can stand in front of a small group and deliver your message with confidence. Ask for (or put yourself on) some presentation skills training if you feel ill-equipped.

3. Start a podcast. This a great, low-cost way of hearing and developing your voice. You could begin by basing your first recordings on your written material and then share it on social media. Another step on from this is to be a guest on someone else's podcast.

4. Attend industry events and conferences and watch other speakers – this will provide you with inspiration and motivation to develop your own style.

5. A good first step at public speaking is to volunteer to do a short talk at a networking group. Most of these are unpaid, and the likelihood is that you'll be offered a short timeslot, maybe 20 minutes or so, but it will enough to allow you to flex and grow your public speaking muscles. You can begin by approaching the organisers of any groups you go to. Again, using some of your writing for inspiration, subject matter and structure is useful to get you started.

6. Once you've delivered some talks at networking groups, then try lifting your gaze to bigger events. This is where your network will work wonders for you. Keep your eye out for calls for speakers and respond to them, and let your contacts know that you're looking for opportunities. As your reputation grows, you may well be approached and asked to speak at conferences too. By this point, you

will need to be a confident and engaging speaker.

7. Use social media to keep an eye out for what your local radio stations are talking about. They frequently use guests – if you see them talking on social media about a topic you know something about, respond to them. There's a chance you'll be asked to talk about it live on air with them.

The world of a professional public speaker who gets paid to speak for a living is very different, and this book isn't covering that arena. However, if you do aspire to grow your speaking skills, then two extremely useful organisations that can support you are Toastmasters and the Professional Speakers Association.

Try this: think about an area or a subject matter that you feel strongly about and in which you would like to become known. Review the ideas above and pick a starting point that you feel comfortable with to launch from. If you're already sharing your ideas and opinions on social media, is it time to start a blog? If you're already an established blogger, maybe it's time to write a white paper or approach an industry journal? Do the same with the speaking ideas – where are you in the pecking order? What's your next step? How are you going to make that happen?

How to Develop a Speaking Success Routine
A few years ago, I gave a talk to a room full of influential businesswomen. It was early on in my career and was a big deal – a chance to demonstrate my knowledge and show leadership in my chosen area, with the hope that further speaking gigs and work would follow.

Except it is a painful memory for me now. Why? My nerves sabotaged me and what should have been a chance to shine, became a lesson in being remembered for the wrong reasons.

From standing with my back to some of the audience (Yes! It makes me cringe now, believe me), to changing my talk at the last-minute and feeling vulnerable and out of control, the innumerable mistakes I made (real and imagined) were replayed for months afterwards. The experience stayed with me for some time. Fast forward a few years, and I can see clearly what went wrong. Happily, I make a much better impression these days!

Our bodies and thoughts can hijack us and undermine our best efforts at putting ourselves across with gravitas and authority – and rob us of our ability to be influential and show leadership, even when we don't have any yet. This is precisely what happened to me. I was at the mercy of my stress hormones and sheer terror set in. It wasn't a pretty sight.

The key is to create a routine that will work for you and support you, ensuring you're in the best possible place physically and emotionally, to get your message across.

Here are nine tips to help you put in place a success routine that will help you present with authority – even if you don't have any.

Before

1. Set your objectives clearly – what do you want colleagues to do after your presentation? Plan the action you want them to take and communicate that clearly. Prepare with enough time. Identify who is going to be there – who are the people you need to connect with and influence?

2. Find your 'why' – what's the reason you're standing in front of the room? Understanding this and being able to articulate it succinctly to yourself as a form of mantra will help focus you and sharpen up your presentation.

3. Make your needs clear. If you need power point, a flip chart or a layout for the meeting, then let that be known

beforehand and ensure the person setting up the room knows about your needs. Make sure you know where you're going to be standing and that everyone can see you!

During

4. Prepare yourself physically. Before you begin to speak, pause and look around the room. Briefly make eye contact with your audience, smile, breathe and check your posture. Make sure you're standing firmly on two feet, and your body language is open. Breathe into your feet as you ground yourself. Own your space with dignity. Make your movements slow, calm and deliberate.

5. Use your voice well. Slow it down, use the deeper end of your voice range (your chest voice) and work to eliminate fillers (the umms and errs) – get used to the sound of silence. Remember to smile.

6. Place the spotlight of your attention firmly on your audience, not yourself. What experience do you want them to have? Keep this in mind as you craft your message – you'll be more focused and connect more with them. Also, understand that people behave differently en-masse. They're difficult to read as an audience, so don't get hung up trying.

After

7. Avoid the confidence-sapping post-mortem by focusing on three things that you know you've done well. Allow yourself one 'Next time I'll change this...' And then let it go...

8. Follow up – initiate contact with key people afterwards.

Influencing upwards means you'll need to talk to those more senior to yourself, which isn't always easy if you hardly see them. Take advantage of the fact they've been in the same room as you. Monitor the impact your presentation has had.

9. Stand your ground. Feedback is vital if we are to grow and develop – but asking for it directly afterwards will dilute the effect you're looking for. Respond positively to any feedback you're offered with a word of thanks and a smile. Resist asking people what they think – you'll appear needy and unsure of yourself. Breathe into your feet, check your posture and smile.

Using writing and/or speaking allows you to demonstrate your expertise publicly. The ideas in this chapter allow you to start small if you want to, and then scale your activity up. The important thing is to start.

Chapter 12

Make Meetings Work for You

"Preparing for meetings is essential. I prepare as much now as I did when I was starting out, religiously looking at everything that needs to be done and then doing a total follow up afterwards."
Tessa Shreeve, CEO of The Luxury Restaurant Guide

Tessa is right – going into a meeting unprepared may be something you can do occasionally, but it's not a strategy for success. It is, however, something I come across with surprising frequency; and people I'm talking to can't fathom why they're not making the impact they want. Why aren't people taking notice of them? Why aren't they in demand? Why aren't they getting picked for the best opportunities?

Meetings are an opportunity to be seen and heard – or not. The choice is yours, so make it the right one. If you're unprepared, it'll be obvious, and you'll impress no one. You can end up feeling very exposed (this is also true of new leaders who have the job of running meetings for the first time – so start gathering examples of best practice before you get to that point).

You may be thinking about meetings with an inward groan of despair. Most organisations have far too many meetings, it's true. Often those meetings drag on for hours with no real purpose and end up being ineffectual. That can be tough. But even in those sterile debating grounds, it's possible to get your voice heard and raise your profile. If you've followed the ideas earlier in the book, hopefully, you'll be involved in the right projects and your time in such environments will be limited – or you'll be looking out for those opportunities.

The ideas in this chapter can be used whether you are in the very early stages of your career and you attend weekly team meetings where all and sundry are present, or whether you're starting to go along to more select gatherings, where you'll meet a range of more influential people. Adapt the ideas to suit your situation, remembering that learning lessons early on in your career will be useful for you as you progress, and those weekly team meetings are an ideal opportunity to try out some of the ideas here.

Meetings (the right ones) are a great opportunity to be in the orbit of influential people. They are a chance to impress, get feedback on your ideas and build alliances. They are also very useful places for watching the dynamics of your team or organisation and understanding the relationships between others. Some careful observation and listening will show you who is really in charge and this will help you to understand who you need to be building relationships with.

What meetings does your boss regularly attend? How do they feel about those? Are there any that they may be keen to get rid of, and would welcome someone else attending in their place? Do they attend meetings that would be an ideal opportunity for you to further your knowledge or raise your visibility? What opportunities are there for you to either go along with them or in their place?

There are three areas to work on: preparation for the meeting, during the meeting itself and the follow-up. All three need thought and attention, and can't be left to chance if you want to use the meeting as a chance to raise your profile.

Preparation for the Meeting

Preparing for the meeting is crucial, and there's lots you can do to lay the groundwork for being more visible.

Nicky Ness has some sage advice to start us off here;

"The more senior I get, the more I learn that you have to nail it! You need to be clear about the problems you're going to solve. Never spend any more than 45 minutes doing it and never have more than six people in the room otherwise it's a nightmare."

Now, some of this advice may be out of your control and influence now, but there are still nuggets of gold here.

Firstly, you'll need to 'nail it' at any stage of your career. This means understanding what the meeting is about and what your input in solving those problems might be. Be clear about these before the meeting and ask questions beforehand if you don't know.

A tremendously useful skill to help you understand the needs and the priorities of the people you're meeting is to be able to cut to the heart of the matter and summarise an issue quickly and succinctly. This talent will help you stand head and shoulders above others for the rest of your career. Practice it frequently. If you can do this, you'll be able to demonstrate to others that you understand their needs clearly and their perspective and you'll have a solid foundation to work from when it comes to being strategic about being seen and heard.

Know who's going to be at the meeting and if you need to, speak to them beforehand. This is a useful thing to do if you've not met them before – that way, you won't be coming to the meeting 'cold'. A quick phone call to introduce yourself where appropriate can work wonders, as can an email.

When you're running your own meetings, Nicky's advice is well worth remembering. Set clear time limits and have a specific focus for the meeting.

Have you ever gone to a meeting not having the read the paperwork beforehand? If so, can you remember what that feels like? It's not a good feeling – panic-inducing is the word I'd use. Don't put yourself in this position. Get prepared to feel prepared. To offer an opinion or share a new idea, you'll need to know what's currently being considered.

Knowledge + an opinion + ideas = visibility.

Look at the agenda. What is the current thinking around those subjects? What different thinking could you approach the subject from? What alternative ideas and viewpoints might be useful to share and what different perspectives are there that might not currently be considered?

Make sure that you have something to say – and if you can have something to say that gives a different angle on the expected viewpoint, so much the better. What questions could you ask? Having a couple of pertinent, prepared questions can be very useful. It demonstrates that you're familiar with the topic and have thought about it.

Another point to consider is what you want to achieve out of the meeting. If you want to go in and get buy-in for an idea, then it's helpful to know your bottom line – what are you willing to walk away with? As Sara Rees says, "Knowing this before you go into a meeting can help you to come out of it having steered your way to the desired outcome. If you've compromised, then it will help you make sure you've not compromised beyond your limits."

Charlotte Sweeney is very organised when it comes to her diary, and I suggest that you learn to take a similar approach.

"Every Sunday I go through my diary for the next couple of weeks, and I make sure I have all my papers ready and that I've read everything I need to read. I make sure I have a view on something so that I can contribute to the meeting and I make sure I diarise planning time to do any work that comes out of the meeting."

Charlotte's advice here about diarising time in for after the meeting is also worth listening to. After every meeting – whether it's a group one, or a 1:1 – allow yourself some time to reflect, make notes, find follow up material and so on. Put this time in your diary as you add the meeting itself, or it won't happen.

Preparing yourself mentally and emotionally for a meeting is just as important. How do you want others to perceive you in that meeting? What is it that you want to achieve and how do you need to show up to manage that?

Jackie Daniel has a great routine for doing this.

"I rehearse. I step through mentally what's going to happen. I prepare in every sense – including emotionally if I know it's going to be a difficult meeting. I think about how I'm going to get myself looking and feeling in the right space, setting the tone of the meeting from the beginning. What do I want to look like as I start opening it, what's the intonation in my voice, what's my body language saying?"

These are points that you can begin to consider too. If you want to use a meeting to raise your profile, you'll need to know what you want people to see in you. Considering your non-verbal communication is a big part of this. If you want to be visible, then ensure that your posture is upright and open, that you're taking up space (not sitting hunched over) and that you're making eye contact with the chairperson.

Rehearsing what you want to say out loud is incredibly useful – particularly if you're planning on making a controversial point. It helps if the first time you say the words out loud, isn't in the meeting, in front of others.

Finally, building allies before a meeting is a marvellous way of helping you to raise your profile and get your voice heard. If you have an idea that you want to put forward, then sometimes it's useful to have someone more influential to support you, particularly if you're just starting out or there's a chance that other people at the meeting may simply not listen. This is being strategic – often ideas need more than one person to get carried through.

During the Meeting

Arrive early so that you get a chance to speak to the other attendees – it helps build relationships if you get to know them as people, so take this time to practice your small talk skills and show an interest in them.

If you've done your preparation, then you'll have something

to say, questions to ask and a point to make, preferably one that's unique and all your own. It's important that you say something, and that what you have to say adds value. You don't want to open your mouth for the sake of it – but equally, think about what you can say that will make you look intelligent and informed.

Jayne Mitchell thinks part of the way to speak up successfully in meetings is knowing when to do so. "Make sure the chair knows you have a point to make. Making one or two short, sharp, to the point contributions is more memorable than making lots of contributions and lots of points. It's knowing when to speak up. I don't allow people to speak over each other – catch the eye of the chair so they know you have a point to make and don't try and push your point over the point of someone else or you'll get drowned out, even if it means going back to a point."

As we've already seen with Heather Melville's example in a previous chapter, one of the biggest challenges for a woman in a meeting can be the tendency to be interrupted, talked over or ignored. A good, strong chair, like Jayne, who runs meetings well will be the perfect antidote to this. Sadly, these can be few and far between, so you'll need to have a strategy for overcoming these behaviours if they rear their ugly heads.

The Cheryl Sandberg and Adam Sandler articles in the New York Times contain some excellent advice, including forming alliances with other colleagues and pledging to support each other if you notice that you're being interrupted or talked over.

Dealing with interruptions can be daunting to cope with. Often the other person may simply railroad over you, and it can take a strong response to pull the conversation back to yourself.

I once worked with a senior manager who had this problem in the engineering organisation she worked for. We developed an approach that worked for her, and she put it into practice as soon as possible after our coaching session.

In the first meeting, as she was talking her colleague talked over her. She asked him to stop and let her finish, but he carried on, and her contribution was lost.

In the second meeting, she asked him to stop and let her finish in a louder voice, while at the same time raising her hand in his direction. He stopped.

In the third meeting, she raised her hand in his direction – and he stopped.

Now, it has to be said that this was a strong approach, developed specifically for her situation, and it's not one I'd recommend across the board. You'll need to make your own judgement as to what will work for you, but similar principles will apply.

If you're being interrupted, take a deep breath and continue talking. Speak slightly louder than normal (but don't shout). If you stop speaking, it gives the other person a green light to go ahead, as does making eye contact for any longer than it takes to say 'let me finish'. Use an appropriate gesture if necessary – if a hand in their direction feels too strong, sometimes just stretching your arm across the table in their direction can have the same effect.

Keep your eyes on the chair of the meeting or whoever you are addressing at that point, and lean in slightly towards them, focusing your energy towards them, not the interrupter.

Carol Rosati encourages women to take ownership at meetings. "If another individual has taken your idea, take ownership and say something like 'I'm glad you think my idea is a good one.' You have to put your head above the parapet and not be so nice – but with humour, so you're not seen as aggressive."

After the Meeting

Following up after a meeting is a huge opportunity to raise your profile – and because so few people bother, it can really boost your visibility and impress others as Tiffany Hall points out,

"The efficiency with which people pick up on actions and get back to you afterwards is always very impressive when people are very strong with that."

Actions from meetings tend to get lost or ignored, particularly after badly run meetings. Be organised, follow up on agreed actions and initiate some contact as soon as possible after a meeting, always ensuring that you have a good reason for doing so.

Some of the following ideas may seem a little daunting if the person concerned is far more senior to you, so pick approaches that you feel comfortable with – but the important thing is to pick one! It's worth remembering too that sometimes it pays to be bold. People are surprising – even the busiest, most senior colleagues may respond to a genuine approach if it's authentic.

Before the meeting, you diarised some time – now is the occasion to use it. Spend a while reflecting on the outcomes of the meeting, what you have learned, what the relationships are like between other attendees so that you get a lay of the political ground, and what needs to happen next. What have you agreed to do and what other actions is everyone else responsible for?

Beverly Smith sees being proactive after a meeting as part of her influencing strategy.

"I've used this in meetings where I've previously not been. I was asked to represent a chief executive on an emergency planning forum. I'd never been asked to do it before, but it was of real interest to me and a great opportunity to make sure I was known. If you're looking for another job, those chief execs are the people to give you one! After that first meeting, I think about things that I might want to touch base with people on and contact them. We meet people all the time – when you get a follow-up email, that meeting becomes a person, a contact and they become part of your network."

Is there someone in the meeting that you feel would be good to get to know a little more – someone who's radar you wouldn't mind being on? This part of the process is all about relationship building, so it's important that you are genuine in these requests.

1. Identify a key person from the meeting and send them an email, refer back to something they said, ask them a question, thank them or point out the impact their contribution to the meeting had on you.

2. Pick up the phone and do one of the above.

3. Send them a link to a relevant article.

4. Ask them if they have any further reading material around the topic they spoke about or their area of interest.

5. Ask to buy them a coffee – this is perhaps in conjunction with one of the other points in the list. In this case, it's important to have a reason – what would you like to know more about? Is there a possibility that this person could develop into a mentor for you? Are they in a role that you aspire to, and would they be willing to share a few words of wisdom with you about how their career has panned out? You'll need to know why you want to meet them – but once you do, it's worth trying this approach to raise your profile with them.

6. Introduce them to someone who would be a good connection for them.

7. Offer to help someone with their actions from the meeting – particularly if it's a project that you'd like to become involved in or you feel you have specific skills that would be useful, or maybe you'd like to develop skills or gain expertise in this area.

8. If they're on social media, follow them and interact with them.

My key message to you in this chapter is don't waste your opportunities. Let's end the chapter with another message from Tessa Shreeve.

"You need to take people on a journey. Use every touch point in your communication to paint a picture of who you are and how you work, and bring others along with you – from preparing for the meeting, during the meeting, the delivery and the follow up afterwards."

Chapter 13

Using Feedback

"Feedback is crucial as you can't have development without it. Just being aware of the impact you have on the people around you and building self-awareness is an important quality. It comes from asking the right questions. Ask good questions, and the quality of the feedback is more useful."

Sara Rees, Head of Fundraising at Rays of Sunshine Children's Charity

If you want to grow and develop in your career, then you will need to get good at eliciting good quality, helpful feedback. This, however, can be something of a challenge and like some people I meet, you may be scared of being told what others think about you. The problem is, we can vastly underestimate our achievements and skills and overestimate the things that go wrong, or else we're not aware of how we're coming across to people or how they view us. This is particularly important in leadership, especially if you're after a new role, do others see you as a leader? How can you find out? By asking others, you'll also find out what roadblocks may be in your way.

As Heather Melville acknowledges, "Feedback is an emotive thing in the UK; it's something we're uncomfortable with whereas in other countries it's expected. Feedback is the best learning curve anyone can have and the cheapest market research you can get!"

Feedback can serve a useful purpose, not only in helping us to shed light on blind spots and reveal out talents, but to help raise our profiles too.

"...because when you ask for feedback, you not only find

out how others see you, you also *influence* how they see you. Soliciting constructive criticism communicates humility, respect, passion for excellence, and confidence, all in one go." *Finding the Coaching in Criticism, Harvard Business Review, January/February 2014.*

One of the ways to get comfortable with asking for feedback is to make sure that you're asking the right people – so you're communicating all of the above to those that hold influence – and that you're asking the right questions.

By asking for feedback about your current performance and how you can improve your future performance, you can also make it very easy for your boss to do their job properly, in supporting you as you move through your career. It's often giving feedback that some leaders find tricky. By giving them an opportunity to have this conversation, you're making this job easier for them. Tiffany Hall recognises this "In a past role, my boss and I started asking each other a set of questions. It pays dividends – it's a very constructive piece of dialogue. If I ask for feedback proactively, it helps him to do his job."

So, what stops us from asking for feedback and why is it such an emotive issue?

Often, it's to do with a bad experience in the past that we can't get out of our heads. The longer we hold onto it, the more reluctant we are to embrace feedback. However, it's important to make the distinction between solicited and unsolicited feedback. What I'm talking about in this part of the chapter is proactively soliciting feedback that will help you to grow. As Carol Rosati says, "...you may not want to listen, but you need to hear it."

How do you do this?

Pick the Right People

This isn't about accepting the opinions of everyone who may be waiting for an opportunity to metaphorically stick the knife in or get one over on you. Motivation is important. You need to pick people who have your best interests at heart and who want to see you succeed. This doesn't mean that you'll be getting feedback that's through rose-coloured glasses. Alongside this, you'll need to pick people that are bold enough to be honest with you. This can become a problem as you grow in seniority – it's often not easy to tell the boss exactly what you think or levy criticism at them, so if you build a group of trusted people around you now, you'll have them well-versed in this by the time you land your CEO role!

If you've read the chapter on finding an advocate and/or a mentor, this person may well be the type of person you could ask.

During a workshop years ago, a delegate told me a story about some early feedback they had received. It had hurt – really hurt. But, it came from a place of love for them and as such, they were able to accept it. This is what you are aiming for.

Get Your Timing Right

Asking for feedback too often can make you seem needy, so it's a good idea to have a plan in place for the frequency with which you'll ask for it. Two or three times a year may be enough, or perhaps after the completion of a major piece of work if there's something specific you want to understand about your performance.

Ask the Right Questions

'So how am I doing?' is rarely going to give you the feedback you need. It's too vague and unstructured, and the person attempting to answer it may not know where to start. If you've ever been given feedback of the 'it was OK, you were good,' variety, I'm guessing it's likely to be in response to a question like the one above.

To get useful feedback that will help you to improve your

performance and raise your profile, you need to be specific. You need to know what you are doing well, and what you can do to improve. And it's effective to limit those pieces of information too.

Two suggested questions are:

What one thing do you see me doing really well?
What one thing would help me improve?

You may want to tweak the wording of the questions, but the answers to these are the information that you're looking for. They are both positively-phrased, forward-looking questions that will inform your current performance and help you improve your future one. The second question isn't about seizing on past failures, real or imagined, and taking you to task over them, but is about isolating one aspect of your behaviour, attitude or the way you show up, and helping you to understand how to make it work more in your favour.

The right person (or people), the right timing and the right questions will help you to raise your profile by asking for feedback – and improve your performance at the same time.

And if you're in any doubt about the importance of feedback, consider this quote from Carol Dweck, author of Mindset – The New Psychology of Success;

"It's easy to surround ourselves with people who make us feel good, but think about it, do you never want to grow? Next time you're tempted to surround yourself with worshippers, go to church. In the rest of your life, seek constructive criticism."

Wise words indeed.

Deal With It Well

Not all feedback is easy to digest. Even positive feedback can be difficult to accept – one of the advantages of asking more than one person is that you'll get a range of opinions and it's harder to ignore it if the same themes keep coming up. At some point, you will need to decide to accept the feedback you're given and choose to believe your peers, colleagues or boss when they tell you what you're doing well. Rejecting their opinions in this situation is like saying 'I don't trust you, you've got bad judgement' – and just take a minute to reflect on that.

Are you really saying that your boss's positive feedback about you is a lack of judgement on their part? Honestly? While humility is a good thing in a leader (and anyone else), false modesty is ultimately irritating. Learn to recognise your skills and talents by using this process to help you identify them.

If you've picked the right people to ask for feedback, then they will be answering the second question through a developmental lens, and not looking to score points off you or use it as an opportunity to undermine you or sabotage you.

This doesn't mean that the feedback is always going to be easy to hear though, and there will be times that you feel triggered. Going through the whole process with an open mind will help you to deal with it positively. I'd also recommend getting to know yourself well – and I mean the less-than-palatable parts too. This is so important as it will make any feedback easier to judge, both solicited and unsolicited. If you tend to react negatively to any perceived criticism, then recognise this about yourself. Allow yourself some breathing space to calm down and then examine it logically. In the next section, I'm going to take you through a process for examining unwanted, negative feedback, which you may also find useful here.

However, if you consistently get the same feedback about a need to change, or something that's getting in your way, then maybe it's time to examine it a little more closely.

Unsolicited Feedback

One of the dangers of unsolicited feedback is that it can sting like crazy – whether it's true or not. We may tend to dwell on it and ruminate over the details. This stops us from using feedback as a development tool and means we're missing out on the benefits and opportunities to raise our profile.

Many years ago, when my son was small, and I was a single parent, I was given the chance to take part in an exchange trip to New York. I went through a rigorous series of interviews and was the only female selected in a team of five. We spent four weeks in New York City, Westchester County and Staten Island, giving presentations to groups of professionals, as well as having the opportunity to visit the US equivalent of our industries.

On the first night, we asked our team leader, Ken, why he had picked us. He looked at me and said,

"You were my first choice Sue – but a woman on the team thought you had far too much to say for yourself, and how could you possibly leave that little boy?"

At this point, the red mist descended and I felt furious and upset. The next day I saw this as a gift; for the first time in over 30 years, I understood that I didn't have to accept someone else's opinion of me if I didn't want to.

I had sat and thought through what she had said to me and looked to see if there was any truth in it. I spent some time examining various aspects of myself and concluded that the feedback she had given about me was wrong. I was eloquent, confident, used to talking in front of groups and had excellent relationships with colleagues, the parents at the school I taught in, and my peers. I'd never received feedback like that before (and haven't since). The skills she was criticising me for were the very ones I needed in the role I'd been picked for. And my son was very happy staying with his dad and surrogate granny!

This experience helped me to put together a process for dealing with criticism that can help you to gain perspective on what you're hearing. It's important to point out that sometimes there WILL be some truth to it. The better you know yourself, and the more objective you can be, the easier it is to recognise that.

Defensiveness will derail you and stop you making progress.

Responding to Feedback

1. Ask yourself how clear you about what the feedback is saying – do you need to ask any questions to drill down into what the other person is saying about you? Ask them what they mean specifically.

2. The next thing to do is to examine their motives. What's going on here? Why are they giving you this feedback, in this way, at this moment? What's going on for them – and what's in it for them?

3. Ask yourself if there's any truth to it. This is where it's important to know yourself well, and to be objective. You'll arrive at this point over time. It's about accepting all of who you are – even the sides to you that you may wish you didn't have! If you've asked for feedback from others, then you will have something to go on here. Knowing that you're often late for example, can help to take the sting out of feeling criticised if someone levies this at you.

4. At this point, you'll have a yes or no answer – there's some truth to it or not. At this point, you'll need to decide what to do.

5. If it's a yes – what are you going to do, if anything?

6. If it's a no – what are you going to do, if anything?

In my example, I decided that there wasn't any truth to the criticism levelled at me. At that point, there was very little I could do regarding recourse and decided to do nothing. I mentally gave her back the gift of her feedback.

In more recent times, I have received feedback that has stung – not least because after some deliberation; it turned out that, yes, it was fair. One example was around some activities I ran on a training day. The feedback was that they were repetitive; the next day I could see that there was some truth to this, and used the experience to revise the way I planned training sessions and ensured variety.

Once the emotion of receiving the feedback has died down, this is a useful process to work through. And it's even more effective when you talk it through with someone else.

Sharing Feedback About Yourself

I'd like to end this section with some thoughts around sharing feedback that you get about your work, and how to share this with others.

It's an idea that met with a variety of views when I interviewed the women for this book. Some dismissed it out of hand as being a step too far. However, approached in the right way, this can be a key tool in raising your profile amongst your key influencers. It's not about spamming your senior leadership team with daily updates on your work, or random praise, and it's not about emailing distant connections and members of your network out of the blue. It's about letting key people know that you're doing well – sharing what you're doing with them, and most importantly, the impact of that work.

Jackie Daniel considered it a vital tool in keeping people in the loop. She preferred to write a weekly CEO message – "It's my weekly update and it varies from topic to topic. I remember thinking about how on earth I'd keep this up, but I have, no problem – the staff love it!"

Now you may not have a platform as large as a CEO might – but what are the possibilities for you when it comes to initiating a weekly update from your team or department? Do you have updates and news that a wider audience would benefit from? If you're initially reluctant to share your successes, then a good way to start is by sharing your team's.

Sara Rees backs up this point. "Successes can be really motivating, and if you take the time to acknowledge other people and their work and contribution, then that's a really generous thing to do."

Of course, it's important to make sure that you balance this collaborative approach with news about yourself. Karen Friebe has this advice – "You should share updates on your work and its impact otherwise people will overlook you. I tell the women I work with, let me know when a client says something good about you and we'll include it in your performance review and I'll pass it on to the bosses. They must know that you're doing well – and it's not showing off."

This encompasses several points already made in this book. If you've got an advocate, so much the better – they will be ideally positioned to speak up for you. It also highlights how important it is to keep a record of your successes and contributions. It's too easy to dismiss or forget what you've done.

Understand your boss, and then communicate your successes in a way that they will listen to. An email once a month, or a verbal update, will keep you front of mind. If you aren't doing it, you can be sure that someone else will be sharing their successes, and it will be their name that springs to mind when opportunities arise. You need to find whatever works for you and be consistent.

Chapter 14

Get Good at These

As I mentioned in the first chapter, it goes without saying that you need to be excellent at your work and committed to nurturing that excellence through regular professional development. Your professional skills need to be top drawer.

In this final chapter, I share three other skills that I believe will contribute hugely to your presence, raise your profile and help you stand out from the crowd. It's probably no surprise that they are all centred around communication.

Listen So They'll Speak

I find listening to be one of the skills we need most for success in life, and sadly, one of the skills most people possess the least. Who do you know who is a great listener? Who do you know who is a poor listener? The chances are that you found the latter question easiest to answer.

I talk about three levels of listening.

The first is surface listening. This is not really listening at all, but rather, paying scant attention to someone while we do something else. Our mind isn't in the conversation at all; if you've ever listened to a youngster babble on while you're trying to make dinner, this is the kind of 'listening' that you may be displaying. You'll realise after a while that you can't remember a single thing they've talked about.

The second level is conversational listening. This is what we do most of the time. We pay attention up to a point, but mainly because we want to jump in and add our own anecdotes, experiences and generally demonstrate something about ourselves. We're listening to respond rather than truly understand what the other person is saying. In a professional context, it's the listening of point scoring, 'let me demonstrate how good I am', or 'if I don't speak now, I'll miss my chance'. It prevents a true understanding of what is being said because we're mainly working from our own agenda.

Now, in reality, this kind of listening makes the world go around – we take turns, fill in each other's sentences, interrupt, change the topic and so on. It's the bread and butter of listening that we put up with and probably practice ourselves to a large extent.

The third level is deep active listening. This is the type of listening that professional listeners are trained to use – coaches, counsellors, mediators and so on. This is demanding and takes real skill to use expertly. You don't need to be a highly trained expert listener, but there are things you can do to improve how you show up with others, that will enhance the impact you make and help raise your profile.

If you make someone feel listened to, then they won't forget you in a hurry. Listening and being fully present with someone will go a long way towards achieving this. The mnemonic below will help you to improve your skills in this area.

Look interested, get interested – aim to develop an interest in the human being in front of you. Give them your full attention, which means no looking over their shoulder or glancing at your watch or mobile phone.

This is about being fully present for the person in front of you. Just being with them - present moment awareness. Having a head full of 'stuff', our own agenda working in the background, and feeling under pressure ourselves can end up making the person in front of you feel unimportant. This is probably not intentional – but the result is the same.

Keeping your eyes on the speaker is an immediate way showing them that you are fully present. Do be aware of cultural differences here, some cultures regard eye contact as disrespectful, so you'll need to explore other ways of how to listen respectfully.

Your face – be aware of how your face looks as you listen; learn to be interested and respectful of the person in front of you and how to make your face show that. Our body language and facial expressions are largely unconscious, but we can learn how to act intentionally and change long-held habits, and the first thing is to be aware of them.

If you know that your face looks bored or fed up or unfriendly as you speak, then people will react to that. Experiment with changing your expression so you create a different, more engaging and welcoming aura around you - this isn't about sitting there with a false, stiff smile on your face but developing *some genuine curiosity and respect for the person in front of you* and allowing that to show through. How can you look encouraging, for example?

Involve yourself by responding – use small gestures and responses that indicate you are listening. Nods, smiles, murmurs of assent, laughing in the right place all show that your attention is on the speaker.

Stay on topic – do not allow yourself to drift away and ensure any responses you make are to do with what is being said, not nudging the conversation in a direction that you may like it to go in. Listening involves you focusing on the other person, not yourself.

A lack of awareness of other people often causes us to interrupt. We finish people's sentences for them; we get carried away with our own ideas. If you tend to do this, write your idea down and share it afterwards.

Test your understanding – ask questions to ensure you understand what is being said.

Evaluate the message – think carefully about what is being said and use paraphrasing and summarising sentences to encapsulate the heart of the other person's message. A phrase to use might be 'So are you saying that...?' or 'You seem a little frustrated by ...?'

Deep active listening is about recognising the emotions behind the speaker - tentatively, without presumption, allowing them to reflect on how they feel and reiterating their message if needed. You'll hear, "Yes, that's it exactly," which helps them to feel understood - or they'll say, "No, it's not that really, it's more that I'm feeling like this... "

Neutralise your feelings – try not to become emotionally involved. Remain detached and non-judgemental about what you hear, as this will encourage the other person to open-up to you. Remember, it's not about you.

'Listen from nothing' - be aware of your own filters and assumptions that you make about people. Don't dismiss people before they have a chance to speak. Everyone has untapped potential and unplumbed depths than we can possibly know – and you'll never find out about them without a sense of curiosity about that person in front of you. You don't know what you don't know about them.

Speak So They'll Listen

In her recent excellent 2015 HBR article, Nancy Duarte talks about the importance of being able to empathise with your team, investors, customers and the public. *To Win People Over; Speak to Their Needs and Wants* explores examples of how to build a capacity for empathy and then transfer this into your approach to work.

Empathy is fundamental to success as a leader because it allows us to see things directly from another's viewpoint. This means we can be more sensitive in how we communicate. As Duarte says, "If people feel listened to, they become more receptive to your message. And by doing the listening, you become more informed about what they really need – not just what you think they need..."

Speaking 'to their needs and wants' is a key piece of your profile-raising puzzle. To get your message across effectively, you need to be speaking to other people in a language that they will understand and will listen to.

Here are three ways to engage others in productive conversations, which will help you to raise your profile, open-up opportunities and be remembered.

Ask Questions

What gets in the way of asking a great question? The assumption that we already know the answer. So many people go through life with the 'answers' already in their heads that they have no room for the questions that might open-up a conversation, provide a unique viewpoint and help them get to the heart of the matter, so the real issue is uncovered. As I was taught in my coach training, stay with the not-knowing. Open questions that allow others to reflect and think will be the ones that make the most impact – and so will you.

Asking questions not only builds empathy and rapport, but questioning at an operational and organisational level will also bring rewards.

Curiosity might have killed a few cats, but it will help to raise your profile as you become engaged with your environment and the people in it. This skill will help you to look at what's around you with innovative eyes and ask, 'what's possible?'. It will help you to ask questions that unearth hidden truths and uncover stale practices, invigorating relationships and prompting new ways of thinking about 'how we do things around here'. Curiosity is about the new and the different, bringing energy and light to refresh and revitalise teams and organisations. In the workplace, questioning the status quo will earmark you as an innovative thinker. Remember, leaders forge new paths, they don't blindly follow existing ones.

Take Notice of Their Communication Style

Do people glaze over, look bored or impatient when you speak to them? If you're someone whose communication style is to give long, detailed, rambling explanations, then this might be the problem. You may be speaking to someone who prefers concise, crisp information, presented succinctly.

The same will be true in reverse. A big picture person speaking to a detail-driven colleague may not be a match made in heaven.

The onus is on you to understand the style of the person you're speaking to and be flexible enough to match it. And it goes without saying that you need to have something to say that is worth listening to.

It's also worth noting that aiming to be concise (but not unfriendly or abrupt) in your own style will help with the clarity of your message, and is a style favoured by the senior leaders I've met and worked with. We live in a time of information overload, and less really is more. Avoid over-explaining ideas, and know when to stop. Recognise when you have made your point and then be quiet – there's no need to make it several times in different ways or reiterate it to make doubly sure they've got it.

Be prepared, choose your words well, pace yourself and pay attention to your tone of voice. These will set your verbal communication above others and help you to be remembered for the right reasons.

Know their Agenda

Understanding their priorities, what matters to them and where their focus lies will be one of the most successful strategies you have in communicating with others.

A recent client, Muriel, faced a meeting with her immediate

line manager to discuss some upcoming project work. Keen to get her message across about her role, we explored what her manager would listen to. What was guaranteed to get him to prick his ears up? Couching her argument in those terms may be the element needed for success. "It was like I flicked a switch, he suddenly became lit up," she reported back after the meeting. "It was like talking to a different man – amazing."

By using this approach, you are signalling to the other person that you understand what they need too, which as Duarte asserts, "…will fuel your relationship with your stakeholders over the long run."

Be Assertive

Lose the people-pleasing habit. People-pleasing makes it hard to have difficult conversations, accept criticism or cope with others who are less concerned about pleasing you and don't mind how their communication comes across to you. It also makes it a heck of a lot harder to challenge and change, two key skills of a leader that I've already mentioned. People pleasing will simply stop you in your tracks.

Losing the habit may be a challenge; my work with more senior leaders has revealed that this trait can take some time to dislodge itself. I believe that part of the answer to this lies in understanding the true nature of what it means to lead. A leader is a disruptor – as I mentioned earlier in this chapter, they are a path clearer, not necessarily a path follower. Now I'm not advocating civil disobedience, but as a leader, you'll need to be prepared to challenge and change.

Learn to be bold, speak up respectfully, be prepared, well researched and not afraid to fail. Elsewhere in the book I've talked about the challenges women can face when they speak up – but this is no reason to avoid doing it.

Here's a reminder of what it means to be assertive:

Aggressive: my needs matter and yours don't.
Assertive: my needs matter and so do yours.
Passive: your needs matter and mine don't.

Make sure that in any conversation, you go for what's called the 'win-win'. If you understand the others person's agenda, you can match their communication style, you listen well and are focused on a common outcome, then you'll stand a much better chance of getting your views heard.

Raising your profile and being noticed means that not everyone is going to like/approve/agree with you or your decisions. And that's ok – you can live with that. It might feel uncomfortable to begin with, but we get used to everything given time.

This diagram can be useful to help you explore who 'matters' and who doesn't – we all matter as humans, but we can waste far too much time ruminating over the opinions of people who don't impact us.

Who Matters

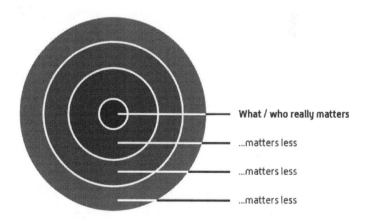

What / who really matters
...matters less
...matters less
...matters less

In the centre of the diagram, write down every person that truly matters. This is where your focus should be – these should be the people you need to be listening to and taking notice of. These could be your family, best friends, key clients, customers, your boss, your team... it's up to you to choose who you put in here.

For the rest of the circles – and add more if you need them – you add people in decreasing importance. People-pleasers tend to focus too much on the outer circles – the wrong ones.

And Finally...

If you have ambitions and goals to reach more senior levels in your industry, then leaving your career to chance simply won't work. Making sure that you are visible, heard and noticed by the people that matter, and engaging with them in a way that they will listen to, will help accelerate your progress. This can feel like a challenge at times. The ideas in this book will give you practical starting points from which to move forward. Whatever level you want to take your career to, learning how to use the 14 ideas and *put them into practice,* will give you a set of tools that you can utilise at every stage of your career. They are versatile and timeless – approaches that every professional, serious about their career trajectory, would do well to get to grips with and use every time they want to shift their role up a gear.

This is, of course, one piece of the puzzle. There is still a lot of work to be done as we strive towards full equality in the workplace, but ensuring that you are getting your voice heard, and your accomplishments noticed, will help perhaps more than you may think. I believe it's going to take a combined approach of tacking outdated cultures and attitudes in the workplace, challenging unconscious bias in everyone (women included) and a monumental effort on behalf of women themselves, in order for us to see change.

Speaking up, being bold and courageous, challenging, sticking your head above the parapet, asking for what you want and refusing to blend into the background – raising your profile involves all of these, and with these behaviours, comes risk. But don't let it put you off! There's strength in numbers – surround yourself with a likeminded tribe of people. One way to do that is to become a shining beacon that attracts others to you.

I'd urge you to show up at work – and in your life – in a way that encourages other women to succeed. Be a role model yourself. Be a mentor, and when the time is right, be a sponsor for another woman. Be supportive.

How do you do that?

Women who support other women do these. They...

- Speak up for other women
- Mentor other women
- Encourage others
- Are kind, helpful and generous
- Genuinely feel happy for the success of others
- Recommend other women
- Promote the success of other women
- Build friendships as well as business relationships
- Champion women
- Compliment them on their achievements not just their appearance

The world is changing for women, albeit at a slow pace. You can make a difference by showing up, making yourself heard and encouraging other women to do the same.

And to finish...

Of course, reading a book is the easy part – the challenge of implementing the ideas comes next! If you'd like some free resources to help you do that, then email hello@susanritchie. co.uk and we'll send you some links!

Further Reading

Here is a list of books you may find useful

The Curse of Lovely - Jacqui Marson

Daring Greatly - Brene Brown

Mindset: The New Psychology of Success - Carol Dweck

Personal Impact - What it takes to make a difference - Vickers, Bavister, Smith

Finding Peace in a Frantic World - Danny Penman and Mark Williams

Compelling People - The Hidden Qualities That Make Us Influential - John Neffinger and Matthew Kohut

Brave - Margie Warrell

The Power of Nice - How to Conquer the Business World with Kindness - Linda Kaplan and Robin Koval

The 7 Habits of Highly Effective people - S R Covey

Feel The Fear And Do It Anyway - Susan Jeffers

Influence - Robert Cialdini

Supercoach - Michael Neill

Time To Think - Nancy Kline

Embodied Leadership - Pete Hamill

Brilliant Coaching - Linda Starr

Presence - Amy Cuddy

Lean In - Sheryl Sandberg

Gravitas - Caroline Goyder

The One Minute Manager - Kenneth Blanchard and Spencer Johnson

Emotional Intelligence - Dr David Walton

The FT Guide to Networking - Heather Townsend

Bibliography

Books

Embodied Leadership – Pete Hamill

The Financial Times Guide to Networking – Heather Townsend

Mindset: The New Psychology of Success – Carol Dweck

A Woman in Your Own Right – Ann Dickinson

Reports

The importance of social capital for breaking the glass ceiling – Natasha Abajian, City University, London, January 2016 https://www1.bps.org.uk/system/files/user-files/DOP%20 Annual%20Conference/dop_2016_abstract_book_web.pdf

Women Matter: Gender Diversity, a corporate performance driver – McKinsey and Co, October 2007 https://www. mckinsey.com/business-functions/organization/our-insights/ gender-diversity-a-corporate-performance-driver

Women on Boards Report – HM Government, 2013, 2015 update https://www.gov.uk/government/collections/women-on- boards-reports

Articles

Speaking While Female – New York Times, Sheryl Sandberg and Adam Grant, January 2015 http://www.nytimes. com/2015/01/11/opinion/sunday/speaking-while-female. html?_r=1

Why Women Don't Apply for Jobs Unless They're 100% Qualified – Tara Sophia Mohr, Harvard Business Review, August 2014 https://hbr.org/2014/08/why-women-dont-apply-for-jobs- unless-theyre-100-qualified

The Innovation Mindset in Action – Vijay Govindarajan and Shrikanth Srinivas, Harvard Business Review, August 2013 https://hbr.org/2013/08/the-innovation-mindset-in-acti-3

Find a Sponsor Instead of a Mentor – Sylvia Ann Hewitt, Forbes, September 2013 https://www.forbes.com/sites/danschawbel/2013/09/10/sylvia-ann-hewlett-find-a-sponsor-instead-of-a-mentor/#21c459311760

We Don't Need a hero, We Just Need More Women at the Top – Gayle Peterson, The Guardian, November 2013 https://www.theguardian.com/women-in-leadership/2013/nov/13/more-women-at-the-top

To Win People Over, Speak to their Needs and Wants – Nancy Duarte, Harvard Business Review, May 2015 https://hbr.org/2015/05/to-win-people-over-speak-to-their-wants-and-needs

The Authenticity Paradox – Herminia Ibarra, Harvard Business Review, January 2015 https://hbr.org/2015/01/the-authenticity-paradox

A secret weapon businesses underutilize – CBC Network, March 2016 https://www.cnbc.com/2015/02/17/how-businesses-can-tap-an-underutilized-weapon-women.html

Ted Talk

Your Body Language May Shape Who You Are – Amy Cuddy, June 2012 https://www.ted.com/talks/amy_cuddy_your_body_language_shapes_who_you_are

About Susan Ritchie

Susan brings decades of teaching experience to her work as a writer, executive coach and trainer. In 2002, Susan left the UK to move to Borneo with her then nine-year-old son. As a single mum, she taught in South East Asia for five years, followed by three years in Central America. She quickly learned to establish herself in a country where she knew no one, and set about building her reputation, network and career. Returning to the UK in 2010, she set up her consultancy, where she now helps ambitious professionals to develop their leadership identity and presence, making their mark professionally. Her practical, common-sense approach has earned her an international client base which spans both the public and private sector, and includes the BBC, The Institute of Chartered Accountants, Tower Hamlets Homes, charities, schools and universities.

More information about Susan's work, including her talks and workshops, can be found at www.susanritchie.co.uk.

A note from Susan Ritchie

I do hope that you've enjoyed reading this book, as much I enjoyed writing it and hearing the inspiring stories from the women I interviewed. If you have a few moments to add a review to your favourite online review site, that would very much appreciated. If you'd like to keep up to date with my next book, blogs, talks and workshops, you can sign up at my website www.susanritchie.co.uk, where you'll also find a range of free resources.

I would also love to hear how you get on with the ideas. You can contact me in the following ways:

Email: hello@susanritchie.co.uk

Twitter: @susanjritchie

LinkedIn: www.linkedin.com/in/susanritchie1

Previous Titles

Strategies for Being Brilliant: 21 Ways to be Happy, Confident and Successful ISBN 978-0-904327-16-8

In 2002, Susan moved to Borneo with her young son. Now, this might not be your cup of tea, but if self-doubt stops you from having what you want, then this inspiring and engaging book will help you to 'get out of your own way'. Susan shares practical ideas and ways of thinking that will help you to be happier, more confident and successful, whatever the situation.

Praise for Strategies for Being Brilliant

"As a bit of a personal development junkie it's sometimes frustrating to find so many books rehashing the same sort of advice. Fortunately, Sue Ritchie's book is like a breath of fresh air. Sue combines smart, practical strategies to increase confidence and happiness with her own compelling story."

"Sue's talent lies for me in blending her down to earth approach with a wealth of personal and professional knowledge which not only convinces the reader that they CAN be successful, it is also full of accessible and useful hints, tips, revelations and ideas for HOW."

"This is the perfect book for anyone who's always wanted to let their brilliance shine, but didn't know how to. Sue Ritchie's strategies are simple, practical tips which are easy to implement and yet help to facilitate real change. Warning: brilliance may follow!"

"This is a great book that delivers just what it promises. The book is split into 21 sections, each of which explores a simple suggestion for how you can take control and build a satisfying and successful life. The author speaks from experience using her own interesting life as a case study. The book has a straightforward no-nonsense approach and is enjoyable and easy to read. It left me fired up and ready to effect change!"

"Susan's book is required reading for anyone looking for practical ways to overcome life's curve balls'. The 21 Strategies for Being Brilliant are steeped in Sue's deeply moving personal experiences and are superb at reminding us all that WE have the power to change and to choose how we respond to situations."

"With a common touch that will appeal widely, Susan has written a warm and practical self help guide through the lens of her personal and professional journey. Peppered with her experiences as a teacher, coach, business owner, single mum and intrepid traveller, she delivers a wealth of insights and strategies for taking action that will genuinely enhance your life."

**BUSINESS
BOOKS**

Business Books

Business Books publishes practical guides
and insightful non-fiction for beginners and professionals.
Covering aspects from management skills, leadership and
organizational change to positive work environments, career
coaching and self-care for managers, our books are a valuable
addition to those working in the world of business.

15 Ways to Own Your Future
Take Control of Your Destiny in Business and in Life
Michael Khouri
A 15-point blueprint for creating better collaboration, enjoyment,
and success in business and in life.
Paperback: 978-1-78535-300-0 ebook: 978-1-78535-301-7

The Common Excuses of the Comfortable Compromiser
Understanding Why People Oppose Your Great Idea
Matt Crossman
Comfortable compromisers block the way of anyone trying to
change anything. This is your guide to their common excuses.
Paperback: 978-1-78099-595-3 ebook: 978-1-78099-596-0

The Failing Logic of Money
Duane Mullin
Money is wasteful and cruel, causes war, crime and dysfunctional feudalism. Humankind needs happiness, peace and abundance. So banish money and use technology and knowledge to rid the world of war, crime and poverty.
Paperback: 978-1-84694-259-4 ebook: 978-1-84694-888-6

Mastering the Mommy Track
Juggling Career and Kids in Uncertain Times
Erin Flynn Jay
Mastering the Mommy Track tells the stories of everyday working mothers, the challenges they have faced, and lessons learned.
Paperback: 978-1-78099-123-8 ebook: 978-1-78099-124-5

Modern Day Selling
Unlocking Your Hidden Potential
Brian Barfield
Learn how to reconnect sales associates with customers and unlock hidden sales potential.
Paperback: 978-1-78099-457-4 ebook: 978-1-78099-458-1

The Most Creative, Escape the Ordinary, Excel at Public Speaking Book Ever
All The Help You Will Ever Need in Giving a Speech
Philip Theibert
The 'everything you need to give an outstanding speech' book, complete with original material written by a professional speech-writer.
Paperback: 978-1-78099-672-1 ebook: 978-1-78099-673-8

On Business And For Pleasure
A Self-Study Workbook for Advanced Business English
Michael Berman
This workbook includes enjoyable challenges and has been designed to help students with the English they need for work.
Paperback: 978-1-84694-304-1

Small Change, Big Deal
Money as if People Mattered
Jennifer Kavanagh
Money is about relationships: between individuals and between communities. Small is still beautiful, as peer lending model, microcredit, shows.
Paperback: 978-1-78099-313-3 ebook: 978-1-78099-314-0

Readers of ebooks can buy or view any of these bestsellers by clicking on the live link in the title. Most titles are published in paperback and as an ebook. Paperbacks are available in traditional bookshops. Both print and ebook formats areavailable online.
Find more titles and sign up to our readers' newsletter at
http://www.jhpbusiness-books.com/
Facebook: https://www.facebook.com/JHPNonFiction/
Twitter: @JHPNonFiction